What To Do When Your Loved One Dies

Step-by-Step Practical & Legal Guide

Fulfill Your Loved One's Last Wishes and Find Your Own Inner Peace

George Koons III, Esq.

PUBLISHING LTD

D1082419

First Edition 2023

ISBN 979-8-9877187-0-4

Written, published, and printed in the United States of America

JOIN THE TEAM

By subscribing to my newsletter, you'll get access to the Team Section of my website, which includes free helpful resources, giveaways, and more. The Team is always the first to hear about my new books and publications.

See the back of the book for details on how to sign up.

About the Book

Coping with the loss of a loved one but need to know what practical and legal steps to take? Follow me as I show you step-by-step how to tackle these issues in a concise and straightforward manner. Together we'll fulfill your loved one's last wishes and bring you inner peace as well.

While hiring legal counsel isn't always an option, you don't have to go it alone. I'm an award-winning attorney and Marine Corps veteran but when my mother died unexpectedly, I found I couldn't handle the loss – practically or legally. After my own journey of discovery, I vowed to help others navigate the turmoil surrounding a loved one's death. By following my breakthrough step-by-step guide, you'll be able to finalize your loved one's estate with minimal stress.

Inside *What to Do When Your Loved One Dies*, you'll find your roadmap for conquering the practical and legal tasks that need to be done, and discover:

- What to do before and after your loved one's passing, tips, and common mistakes to avoid
- How to accomplish practical tasks, plan the funeral, notify creditors, and other matters
- Whether to open probate and how to do it
- How to uncover your loved one's assets and debts and value the estate
- How to pay debts, taxes, distribute assets, and close the estate
- Checklists, and sample notices to keep it simple and you on track

What to Do When Your Loved One Dies is your step-by-step practical and legal guide for managing tasks and tying up loose ends after the loss of a loved one. If you're a loved one or executor that wants it straight, then you need *What to Do When Your Loved One Dies* in your corner.

This book is dedicated to the many people who need practical and legal guidance during a time of great loss. You can do this!

* * *

In Memory of Eddie Garcia and the courage within.

Contents

Introduction

You Can Do This!

The death of a loved one is inevitable and certain to be one of the most difficult times of your life. It's impossible to take away the grief, loss, and other emotions you experience when a loved one dies. It's possible, however, to understand and manage the numerous tasks and responsibilities related to your loved one's death.

This book's purpose is to lessen the practical burdens faced by a loved one or executor at a time of great loss. I will clarify and coach you through the legal, financial, and practical tasks that need to be done when a loved one dies; when they need to be done; and how to do them. In a concise and simple manner, I will give you the ammunition and confidence necessary to perform the tasks that lie before you.

Think of this book as your roadmap for completing these tasks, many of which need to be carried out quickly and accurately. Think of me as your navigator, coach, ally, and professional guide, helping you steer through this difficult time. You aren't in this alone. Together we'll accomplish what your loved one needs you to do.

Chapter 1

The Loss of a Loved One

My mother died when she was 72 years old. She had been in good health, wasn't overweight, didn't smoke, rarely drank, and exercised regularly. I was 39 years old and not prepared for her death—not even close.

She had been sick with pneumonia for a short time when my oldest sister called and told me my mom was on a ventilator. The significance of that statement escaped me. I thought the ventilator was a short-term treatment that would help her recuperate more quickly. During the next few days, my mother's condition didn't improve, and my sister urged me to get on a plane and come immediately. Even as I flew east from Colorado, I was certain I could "will" my mom off the ventilator and back to good health. I never got the chance.

When I arrived at my parents' house, my oldest brother, two sisters, and father were sitting down to dinner in the dining room—the stage that consumed my childhood Sunday afternoons. The dining room was our family's meeting place, where we whined about our teachers, sat amazed at my brother's stomach capacity, and thought life would never end. But that night, we talked about my mother, the days leading up to her hospitalization, and the need for mechanical ventilation to keep her breathing. As we ate, I had a strange experience best described as a rush of emotion, adrenaline, and extreme impatience. I needed to see my mom—now.

When we arrived at the hospital's intensive care unit (ICU), a nurse nervously asked us to sit in a small waiting area overlooking the ICU. I thought it strange that she didn't take us straight back to see my mother. It wasn't long before I noticed doctors and nurses rushing around one corner of the ICU, their voices raised and urgent. My stomach sank. Somehow I knew it was my mom.

A few minutes later the doctor came out, looking like an actor on a TV show. His head was lowered and his expression devoid of encouragement. This wasn't going to be good. Exactly what the doctor said is a blur, but the bottom line wasn't—my mother had passed away. In shock, I said my final goodbyes to my mom as she lay motionless on the hospital bed. I will never forget the warmth of my mother compared with the sterility of the bright, curtained ICU cubicle. She still looked so young and beautiful to me. How could this be happening?

In the days after my mom's death, all rational thought was lost. I was consumed with my own emotions and incapable of helping my father, who was devastated by the loss of his wife. When I was young, cancer unexpectedly claimed an aunt and uncle, and both of my grandfathers had passed away before I was born. But I enjoyed the longevity of my grandmothers well into their 80s and 90s. I expected my mom to live that long. I thought I would have plenty of time to talk to her about my future, family plans, and how much she meant to me. I thought she would be there for me, always available for advice when needed.

In retrospect, despite our extreme and sudden loss, it could have been worse. Thankfully, my older siblings and their spouses were available for support and guidance. My brother-in-law had experienced the death of his parents a few years earlier. He grounded us and kept us on task. There were many things we needed to do—things I had never contemplated.

Chapter 2

You Need a Roadmap

Having experienced the death of my mother—and my father several years later—I've come to understand the unique challenges and demands a loved one's passing places on family members, particularly the executor, the person who manages the loved one's estate and ultimately distributes property to heirs or beneficiaries. If you're this person, it's essential to have the proper frame of mind and a clear, concise roadmap of your journey.

Your Mental Roadmap

Understand that you're on a selfless mission to finalize your loved one's last wishes and clean up any related messes. It's a true act of love, respect, and kindness. Make no mistake about it, you won't be showered with praise or hailed as a hero. In fact, you may be pressured, second-guessed, and criticized by people close to you. Regardless, stay focused on the task at hand, keep the momentum going, and before long you'll accomplish your mission. It will be an achievement you'll be proud of for the rest of your life. Always keep in mind that you're doing this because it needs to be done, and you were the one chosen to get it done. In addition to maintaining this mindset—your mental roadmap—you'll need a physical roadmap to reach your destination.

Your Physical Roadmap

The size and complexity of your loved one's estate will determine your physical roadmap—the route you'll travel and the number of stops you'll make along the way to settling your loved one's affairs. There may be times when you run into a roadblock and are forced to take a side road, requiring a slower pace. There also will be times when you can pull into the express lane and travel at higher speeds to make up for lost time. The point is that you'll likely encounter obstacles—personal, financial, and legal—that need to be resolved before you reach your destination. But they are only obstacles. Together, we'll navigate through these obstacles until your loved one's wishes have been carried out and the loose ends are tied up.

If you're lucky, advanced warning of your loved one's death will give you some time to prepare. In the next chapter I will show you how to use that time wisely. But before we move on, let's consider what's to come.

The Big Picture

The remainder of this book will show you step-by-step how to accomplish the tasks that need to be done during the last days of your loved one's life, immediate tasks to be done after your loved one passes, how to decipher the will, and how to understand the executor's role and determine beneficiaries. I will show you what you need to know about probate; how to open the estate and probate; how to discover your loved one's assets, debts, and creditors; and how to value the estate. You'll learn how to protect your loved one's assets and identity, open a bank account for the estate, obtain an employer identification number, file certain forms with the Internal Revenue Service, and accomplish other practical tasks. I will guide you through notifying creditors, social security, insurance companies, the public, and others about your loved one's passing as well as how to cancel and delete various accounts. Then I will show you how to pay your loved one's debts and taxes, create a plan to distribute your loved one's assets, distribute those assets, perform a final accounting, and obtain permission from the probate court to close your loved one's estate and probate.

Using This Book

I wrote this book to help executors and family members understand and accomplish the many tasks that may arise after a loved one's death. Because many issues correlate to each other, it's best to read the entire book. It will teach you what to expect after a loved one's passing, what questions to ask, and what tasks to perform. It will put you in control. Depending on your loved one's estate and your level of motivation, confidence, and proficiency, the book will help you perform many, if not all, of the tasks yourself. Nonetheless, the guidance in this book is limited, and everyone's circumstances are different. There is no one size fits all format for handling matters after a loved one's death. Issues related to a loved one's minor children, guardianship, trusts, and other matters aren't addressed. Be aware that there are numerous deadlines set by the probate court and state law, and there may be times when you need a probate attorney, accountant, or other professional's assistance. Don't hesitate to seek such professional advice.

To help simplify and accomplish your tasks, the Appendix at the back of the book includes various forms, including an Executor's Checklist, an Inventory List, a Debt Form, and sample notices to creditors and others. Also included is a Glossary of relevant legal terms. The Appendix does not include sample court forms due to their length. However, they are available on my website, https://www.georgekoons.com/subscribe, which can be accessed by subscribing to my newsletter. The sample notices and court forms will give you an idea of the information included in a typical notice and court pleading. Although you may be able to use them to prepare your own notices and form pleadings, they aren't tailored or specific to your matter. States and probate courts have different rules and requirements, depending on your county and state. Most probate courts have specific forms tailored to their court, and you should obtain and use the court forms from the probate court applicable to your situation.

Tips and Common Mistakes

Because you're just starting out on your journey to settle your loved one's estate, this is a good time to talk about some dos and don'ts.

1. Take time to experience the loss of your loved one and to grieve.
2. Take care of yourself, both mentally and physically.
3. Consider that deadlines begin running from the date of your loved one's death. Early on, determine the deadlines set by the probate court and the law of the state where your loved one resided at the time of passing —presumably where any probate proceeding will be opened. Strictly comply with these deadlines. For instance, the state where you intend to open probate will have a deadline by which probate must be opened. Depending on the state, you may be required to open probate as soon as 30 days after the death. Another example is a deadline for notifying creditors of your loved one's death so they can submit claims for payment.
4. Determine notification requirements to interested persons, creditors, and others as required by the probate court and the law of the state where your loved one resided at the time of passing (e.g., notice of opening probate and appointing executor, notice to creditors, etc.). Strictly comply with these notification requirements.
5. Pay close attention to important documents as you come across them for identification of assets and liabilities as well as associated payment deadlines.
6. Stay organized and maintain precise records of your activities as the executor, including the estate's assets and

liabilities as well as payments made on behalf of the estate.

7. Treat heirs fairly and keep them informed of the status of settling your loved one's estate. Good communication helps to avoid unnecessary conflicts, reduces anxiety, and makes the process proceed more smoothly.

8. Protect your loved one's assets by ensuring that certain assets, such as a vacant home, are insured. Also, protect your loved one's identity.

9. Don't pay valid debts until the claim period has ended. Then, pay those debts in order of priority.

10. Distribute remaining assets to heirs only after the claim period has ended and all legitimate debts and other obligations have been paid.

11. Keep your momentum. Performing tasks at a regular, consistent pace makes your job easier and results in accomplishing your goal of settling your loved one's estate faster.

12. Keep in mind that probate isn't as scary as you may imagine. Many probate courts are geared to help people who don't have attorneys by providing many forms and instructions that may be needed during the probate process. Respect court personnel, and they will be your allies.

13. Remember that an executor has a legal fiduciary duty to act as a reasonable, prudent person with the highest ethical standards and in the best interests of the loved one's estate. This means you must keep accurate records, meet all deadlines, protect your loved one's assets, treat heirs fairly, obtain professional advice when needed, and otherwise act responsibly.

14. Don't hesitate to seek legal, tax, and other professional advice as needed.

Practical and Professional Tasks

There are many tasks that need to be done, both practical and professional, in settling your loved one's estate. The bulk of the tasks are practical and require no special expertise. You just need to be organized, persistent with accomplishing the task at hand, and communicative. The professional tasks require a higher degree of precision and relate largely to probate and providing a final accounting of your loved one's estate to the probate court.

As you read about what's involved with the professional tasks, it's up to you to decide whether you can accomplish the tasks on your own or whether you should seek assistance. Your decision will be based on your own unique situation. It's important to evaluate the value, complexity, and potential issues related to your loved one's estate along with your expertise, the time you have available to perform the required tasks, and your support system.

Although the court system may seem intimidating at first, most probate courts provide considerable written information and self-help forms designed to greatly ease your burden. You can access this information with a computer and the internet. With an understanding of your situation, you can determine the extent of the tax, legal, or other counsel you may need to help you settle your loved one's estate.

Although there are many tasks to be performed, they don't have to be overwhelming. We'll take them one step at a time and ride the momentum of each accomplishment. Let's get started!

Chapter 3

Tasks to Do During the Last Days of Your Loved One's Life

My mother's death blindsided me, but I was more prepared for my father's death when it happened several years later. I saw it coming.

My dad had been suffering from dementia that seemed to progress exponentially. He was a World War II radioman who fought overseas with the U.S. Army's 96th Deadeye Division. Not long before his dementia set in, my father told me stories about the war, including one where his platoon landed on Okinawa and seized a hill overlooking the Sea of Japan. On this lookout, he watched kamikaze suicide bombers attack U.S. naval ships, with one Japanese Zero actually going down the exhaust stack of one vessel. These stories took on a life of their own as his dementia worsened, to the point where my dad thought he saw paratroopers landing in our backyard in Colorado.

At that point there was no escaping his mental decline, and I began to plan ahead for the inevitable. His physical health took a turn for the worse when he fell in my driveway one autumn day and broke his hip. It wasn't long before our family was unable to care for my dad and keep him safe in our home.

Within a couple of months of living in an assisted living facility, my dad lost his will to live. Although my father's illness was miserable and sad for everyone in the family, it foreshadowed his death and gave us time to prepare mentally and practically for that day.

When your loved one is near death, take the opportunity to become familiar with some legal and practical issues, along with the associated tasks that need to be performed. The time you spend preparing for the inevitable will help you avoid complications that will cost you time, money, and anxiety down the road. This chapter addresses the practical matters that should be done as soon as possible.

Evaluate Your Loved One's Needs

If your loved one is in a hospital, nursing home, hospice, or similar facility, then most of his or her physical and medical needs are being met by qualified people. Although these caregivers are well intentioned, it's unlikely they can offer your loved one the companionship a family member or other loved one can provide. Be there for your loved one when you can.

It's not easy to watch a loved one's rapid decline, but realize that you're making a big difference even though your loved one may not be able to communicate this to you. During my dad's last weeks in the nursing home, it was difficult for me to visit him. His dementia had progressed to the point where he was not talking, and I could only keep up a one-way conversation so long. Eventually, I figured out that just being there to support my dad was what it was all about. Try to savor those moments.

If your loved one is living in his or her home, or in your home, then your responsibilities will greatly increase. A full- or part-time nurse or qualified caregiver may be necessary to take care of your loved one. Otherwise, the burden will fall on you and your family members to ensure your loved one's medical, nutritional, and other needs are being met. If you haven't done so already, talk to your loved one's doctors and ask them about your loved one's current needs, what their expectations are for the remaining days of your loved one's life, and what you can do to help maintain the quality of your loved one's life.

While you take care of your loved one, don't forget about the quality of your life and the importance of taking care of yourself.

Take Care of Yourself

It's easy to forget about your own well-being when your loved one is close to death because you're so focused on his or her needs, the tasks that must be done, and the emotions related to your loved one's imminent death. Those who do remember to think of themselves sometimes feel guilty doing so.

If nothing else, you need to maintain your own mental and physical health to make the difficult decisions related to your loved one. This means making sure you're eating healthy, getting the right amount of sleep, exercising, taking care of your own medical needs, and keeping tabs on your emotions.

It isn't a sign of weakness to discuss your emotions with others, seek medical advice, and generally think of yourself during this difficult time. It's healthy and shows you recognize how important it is to maintain your own well-being to make the best decisions for your loved one.

Now that we've tended to you, let's find and review the important documents that will provide the roadmap for your journey.

Find and Review Important Documents

The important documents at this stage typically include a living will, also known as an advance healthcare directive, and various medical and financial powers of attorney. The last will and testament is also a key document, and the executor of the will plays a vital role in fulfilling your loved one's final wishes. Because these concerns don't come into play until your loved one passes, we'll talk about the last will and testament and the executor's role in the next chapter.

At this point, we're looking for all documents that direct how your loved is going to be treated in the last days of his or her life. These documents will also state who's going to make the important decisions on your loved one's behalf. We'll refer to these key people as the "decision makers." There may be only one, or there may be several decision makers. One of them may be you. The first step is to find these important documents so you can identify the decision makers.

To begin the search, talk to your loved one about these important documents, including usernames and passwords to his or her accounts as well as where they're located. Obviously, this isn't an option if your loved one lacks the capacity to understand and speak with you. If possible, contact your loved one's attorney. The attorney who prepared the documents will have them on file. The attorney will also be able to direct you to the decision makers your loved one entrusted to make his or her medical and financial decisions while incapacitated or near death.

If your loved one didn't have an attorney who assisted him or her with these important documents, you need to look in all the logical places where they may be. Start with your loved one's home and look in places where he or she would likely keep these documents for safe-keeping. You want to respect your loved one's privacy, but you also need to find out if these important documents exist. Logical places to search include a home office, study, desk, computer, file box, safe, safe deposit box (which may be at your loved one's bank), storage area, or other place where your loved one spent time and kept valuables.

If you find these important documents, review them carefully for the names of the decision makers. Contact these people, explain the situation, and request their guidance. These decision makers are typically family members, trusted friends, or the family attorney. Considering you're reading this book, you're likely one of these key decision makers.

If your loved one previously informed these people about their roles with his or her end-of-life decisions, then little explanation will be necessary. If not, these people will typically step up and assume their responsibilities once they're made aware of the situation. If they don't, the documents will typically name a contingent, substitute, or backup person.

Now let's demystify the living will and powers of attorney so you can understand their impact on your loved one's care and well-being.

The Living Will

A living will is a written document outlining the medical treatment people want to receive when they can no longer express their wishes or give their medical consent for their own treatment. It isn't a last will and testament, nor is it used to leave property or name an executor or a guardian. A living will is commonly referred to as a health care declaration, advance directive, or advanced medical directive. Don't let the name of the document confuse you. What matters is its contents.

If your loved one has a living will, it will explain the type of health care he or she wants to receive when incapacitated and unable to speak. A living will is typically paired with a medical power of attorney, in which your loved one names an "agent" to make health care decisions on his or her behalf. Medical powers of attorney are explained later in this chapter.

Your loved one's living will should contain any wishes he or she has for medical care, including life-prolonging efforts related to the use of cardiopulmonary resuscitation, blood transfusions, a respirator, surgery, medications, and intravenous food and water. Living wills generally come into effect when a physician determines your loved one is in an "end-stage medical condition." This is an incurable, irreversible medical condition that will likely result in death despite continuing medical treatment. Brain death, irreversible comas, and other vegetative states that have no treatments to make your loved one better are examples of end-stage medical conditions.

It's the responsibility of the agent named by your loved one in the living will to ensure your loved one's medical wishes are carried out. This is true even if those wishes conflict with your opinion, the opinions of family members, or anyone else. An exception occurs if your loved one wasn't of sound mind when he or she executed the living will. Otherwise, all mentally competent adults have the right to direct their own medical care, and even to refuse medical care altogether. In some states, including Oregon, Washington, California, Colorado, Montana, New Jersey, Maine, and Vermont, patients have the power to end their suffering with physician-assisted suicide.

What If There Is No Living Will?

What happens when your loved one doesn't have a living will, is in an end-stage medical condition, and isn't capable of describing his or her wishes? Under these circumstances, certain people may declare themselves to be your loved one's health care representatives. These people must be able to show they are a family member or a close friend of your loved one. Sometimes more than one person will want to act as your loved one's health care representative. Current spouses and adult children from prior marriages are given priority. They're followed by adult children, parents, adult siblings, adult grandchildren, and adult close friends, respectively.

The decision of the highest-priority representative governs the medical decisions. For example, an adult child of your loved one would have priority over the loved one's parents. If there's more than one representative in the highest-priority group, then the group votes on the medical treatment. The majority's vote will decide the medical treatment. If there is no majority, then the group needs to determine how the loved one would have wanted to be treated and make a joint decision. If this can't be accomplished, then mediation, arbitration, or a court proceeding may be the only resolution. This approach should be avoided if possible because it's costly and time-consuming—time your loved one likely doesn't have.

Now that you understand the living will and how it may relate to your loved one, it's time to learn about the "power of attorney."

Power of Attorney

A power of attorney, sometimes referred to as a "POA," is a written legal document (it isn't an actual attorney) in which one person (the "principal") appoints another person (the "agent") to perform specific acts or kinds of acts on the principal's behalf. In your loved one's case, he or she would be the principal. The person your loved one has entrusted to exercise certain acts and make decisions on

15

his or her behalf is the agent. If your loved one has executed a power of attorney, he or she has chosen an agent to make certain decisions on his or her behalf. The chosen agent has the legal authority to control the decisions covered by the specific power of attorney given by your loved one. However, the agent's power is automatically revoked upon the death of the principal loved one. Powers of attorney are broken down into general and limited powers of attorney as well as medical and financial powers of attorney.

General Power of Attorney

If your loved has executed a general power of attorney, he or she has given an agent broad authority to act on your loved one's behalf with few, if any, restrictions. Review the language of the power of attorney to determine who your loved one appointed as his or her agent, what event triggers the start of the agent's power, and the scope of the agent's powers as well as any limitations. The agent's powers under a general power of attorney may include the authority to make all financial, medical, and legal decisions on behalf of your loved one. If you aren't the appointed agent under the general power of attorney, you should let the selected agent know of your loved one's condition and that your loved one has appointed him or her with a general power of attorney.

Limited Power of Attorney

A limited power of attorney provides the principal's agent with the limited power to perform certain acts or make certain decisions. The wording of the specific power of attorney will determine the scope of the agent's powers and the certain acts and decision-making with which they're empowered. Medical and financial powers of attorney are the two types of powers of attorneys that typically apply to a loved one near the end of life. An overview of the medical and financial powers of attorneys will allow you to decide who has the authority to make your loved one's medical and financial decisions.

Medical Power of Attorney

Depending on your location, a medical power of attorney may be called a health care power of attorney, health care agent, medical attorney-in-fact, or some other name. They all refer to the legal authority given to the person chosen to make medical decisions on your loved one's behalf when he or she can no longer make such decisions. Most states have approved medical power of attorney forms. The contents of your loved one's specific medical power of attorney will determine the scope of the agent's power to make medical decisions on your loved one's behalf. The medical power of attorney goes into effect when a physician determines your loved one is unable to make decisions about his or her own health care and treatment.

Under a medical power of attorney, the chosen agent will have the right to be informed of your loved one's condition by a doctor and have full access to your loved one's medical records. More importantly, the agent has the power to choose your loved one's course of treatment, including choosing a doctor and hospital as well as the testing, medications, and surgery that may be administered to your loved one. The scope and limits of the agent's powers will be spelled out in your loved one's specific medical power of attorney, so read the document carefully and consult with an attorney if you have any questions. Realize that a medical power of attorney does *not* give the agent authority to make any financial, business, or other decisions for your loved one.

If your loved one does not have a medical power of attorney, his or her current spouse has the legal right to make the medical decisions if the loved one is unable to do so. In the case of a minor, the minor's parents have the legal right to make medical decisions for the minor. Similarly, a legal guardian is responsible for making medical decisions for their "ward," who's often a minor, incapacitated, or disabled.

When my mother was near death, we found and reviewed her medical power of attorney. Although my dad was alive, my mother had appointed my oldest sister, a registered nurse, as her agent/medical power of attorney. As a nurse, my sister was able to understand and explain my mom's current medical condition and future prognosis as well as guide her treatment. My sister also lived near my mom and knew firsthand her past and present medical condition. My sister's history with my mother and training as a nurse helped the rest of us appreciate what we were dealing with, our options, and the decisions we needed to make.

Not everyone is lucky enough to have a nurse or other medical consultant in their family, but don't let that deter you. As your loved one's entrusted agent, you need to learn his or her medical history, current medical state, treatment options, and likely prognosis. Understanding this information will allow you to make the appropriate medical decisions for your loved one. If this means asking the doctors and nurses endless questions to gain this understanding, then that's exactly what you need to do. I recommend you include your siblings and other close relatives in these conversations. Listen to their feedback, questions, and concerns. Try to achieve a consensus. However, remember it's you, as your loved one's medical power of attorney, who wields the decision-making power related to your loved one's medical treatment. The important point is to be well-equipped with the knowledge necessary to make medical decisions that coincide with your loved one's wishes.

Financial Power of Attorney

A financial power of attorney gives your loved one's agent the legal authority to make financial decisions on your loved one's behalf if he or she isn't capable of doing so. Depending on the scope of the financial power of attorney, the agent's authority may be limited to a specific transaction, such as paying your loved one's mortgage, or be broad enough to cover all financial matters. It may cover any real property or personal property owned by your loved one. Real property refers to real estate, including the land and any structures on the land. Personal property means anything that isn't real property, including cash, bank accounts, stocks, mutual funds, retirement accounts, motor vehicles, and personal effects.

Having the power over another person's real and personal property can prove to be too tempting for certain people. Historically, agents are notorious for stealing from their principals. To help solve this problem, many states have enacted strong laws clarifying the agent's responsibilities. Expect your loved one's financial institutions to look closely at the specific powers given to the agent under the financial power of attorney and limit those powers accordingly.

To limit the agent's power, your loved one may have signed more than one financial power of attorney to cover various financial transactions. Each financial power of attorney must be reviewed to determine the agent's identity and the specific powers your loved one gave to the agent. If you aren't the financial power of attorney appointed by your loved one, contact the named agent and inform him or her of your loved one's condition and the agent's designation as a financial power of attorney for your loved one.

Determining Your Loved One's Competency

Your loved one must be mentally competent to sign any power of attorney. This means that when your loved one signed the power of attorney, he or she must have understood the nature of the property owned or controlled, the powers being given to the agent to make decisions, and the person to whom he or she was giving these powers. If your loved one understands these concepts, then he or she is likely mentally competent to sign a power of attorney. If your loved one wasn't mentally competent when he or she signed the power of attorney, then the power of attorney isn't valid and the agent doesn't have the decision-making powers given in the power of attorney.

Next, we'll talk about another task that needs to be done during the last days of your loved one's life—whether his or her body is to be donated.

Anatomical Gifts

Before your loved one's death, it's important to determine if he or she has agreed to donate all or part of his or her body to science. Making this determination before your loved one's death is necessary because little time is available to prepare, transport, and transplant life-saving organs at the time of death.

Your loved one's donation of his or her body is referred to as an "anatomical gift." There are two types of anatomical gifts. The first entails donating the organs for transplants. The second is donating the body for medical research. Gifting one's body is a purely voluntary decision that must be clearly conveyed before an individual's organs are available for transplant. A donor's family doesn't need to consent to the organ donation and has no legal right to revoke the anatomical gift if the donor was at least 18 years old and of sound mind when he or she agreed to the donation. However, depending on the state where your loved one resided at death, a family member or health care agent may give a doctor permission for the donation if your loved one didn't previously indicate he or she wanted to be an organ donor. A minor child's parents or a legal guardian may legally deed or donate the minor's body as an anatomical gift.

There are several ways your loved one may have indicated the intention to donate all or part of his or her body as an anatomical gift. If your loved one has a living will, it will likely outline the nature of any donation, including the part of the body to be donated and the organization receiving the donation. Your loved one may also have completed a donation form specifying his or her organ donation. Another popular and simple way to designate oneself as an organ donor is by checking the organ donor box when applying for a driver's license. A red heart on the driver's license, typically under the person's signature, indicates he or she has agreed to be an organ donor.

The details related to a donation depend on the agreement with the organization to which your loved one intended to donate his or her organs or body. Your next step is to find and review this agreement, contact the recipient organization, and determine the procedure. It shouldn't be considered indifferent or unfeeling to do this while your loved one is alive. To the contrary, it's the proper way to ensure your loved one's donation is carried out in a timely fashion based on his or her wishes. Your preparedness may save or prolong someone else's life.

Your Loved One's Final Hours

Being with your loved one when he or she leaves this world is an honor and a privilege. If you have the ability to share that moment, I urge you to do so. The day my father died I was skiing with my in-laws from out of state. I was their driver and guide and felt obligated to fill the role, although I knew my dad might not make it through the day. We left shortly after dawn for the mountains, and I hoped to make it back in time. On the drive home, I received the call that my dad had just passed away. My oldest brother and his wife were with my dad at the time, so he didn't die alone. And I was able to say my goodbye to him shortly after he passed. Still, to this day, it's one of my biggest regrets. You have to live with your choices, and this is a tough one to live with, so do the right thing and put your loved one first.

Chapter Summary

In this chapter, you've learned new concepts, accomplished base-line tasks, and overcome obstacles, all while experiencing difficult emotions. You've evaluated your loved one's needs, taken care of your own needs, found and reviewed important documents, determined the decision-makers, learned about important powers of attorney and anatomical gifts, and considered the importance of being with your loved one when he or she passes. Keep following the roadmap, and you'll get to the place your loved one needs you to arrive—the point where the estate is finalized.

In the next chapter, we'll discuss and simplify the tasks that need to be done immediately after your loved one passes away. Keep your head up, your mind focused, and your momentum moving forward.

Chapter 4

Immediate Tasks to Do After Your Loved One Passes

This chapter discusses the tasks that need to be done immediately after your loved one's death. I hope you had some time to prepare yourself for this day. Until it comes, you don't know how the loss will affect you. Some people are able to maintain a calmness and clarity that allows them to move forward with little apparent struggle. Perhaps this is the case when a loved one has gone through a long illness or is very old. Other people find themselves incapacitated, like they're enveloped in a thick, suffocating cloud that makes it difficult to think clearly or move forward with the tasks that need to be performed. It's this latter group I especially thought of as I wrote this book, as that group may need more help. It was also my experience.

Experience the Loss, Then Begin Moving Forward

Immediately after the doctor told me and my family my mom died, I felt the world close in around me. The news brought me to a black, narrow tunnel with little oxygen. Time slowed to a near stop. I couldn't think or speak. A glance at my father brought me around. The energy in his face and body was instantly replaced by devastating grief and loss. He became pale, and his clothes hung on him like a scarecrow. I remember every detail of this moment even though my mom died many years ago. In a blink, we had lost our mom and my dad's wife of more than 50 years. I don't know how any person can truly prepare for such a scenario.

After my initial reaction, I just wanted to find a place to shut down and avoid unwanted attention. My next recollection is sitting on the couch in our small family room with three of my siblings and my father. I don't remember how we got to the car, let alone home. But there we were, together, but not complete. Despite our state of shock somebody thought it would be a wise to have a drink. Whenever I see a bottle of Courvoisier, I remember that moment—its fiery taste as the blood flow returned to my body. It was truly medicinal, but it couldn't overcome the numbness brought on by my mom's death.

The next day was a little better, as was the day after that. I was lucky, because I had three siblings and in-laws beside me at all times. We helped each other share the loss and move forward, one step at a time. My brother-in-law had just gone through his mom's passing and got us immediately on task. I didn't welcome this dose of reality but quickly realized there were many things to accomplish in the coming days.

The roadmap in this chapter, and the rest of the book, will guide you through the steps you need to take after your loved one has passed. Follow the map (including the Executor's Checklist in the Appendix) to reduce your stress and help you overcome the obstacles. When possible, enlist family members and close friends to help with certain tasks and provide emotional support.

Pay Attention to Deadlines, Immediate Bills, and Important Documents You Find

It's important that you move forward quickly and carefully. Deadlines may occur based on the date of your loved one's death that will require you to perform some immediate tasks and let others know of your loved one's death. For example, your loved one may have a life insurance policy that requires you to notify the insurance company promptly (within 30 days), and in writing, of your loved one's death. If your loved one had an accident or life insurance policy, check its "notice" provision and mark any deadlines in your calendar. Later in this book (Chapter 9), you'll learn how to notify creditors, social security, insurance companies, the public, and others of your loved one's passing.

Whenever you uncover a deadline, make a calendar reminder of the deadline, and take the necessary steps to accomplish what is required before the deadline. Missing deadlines can be costly, so pay strict attention to them. Along these lines, you'll also uncover important documents related to bank, mortgage, loan, and other accounts. Set these documents safely aside as you come across them to save you time looking for them down the road.

Later, in Chapter 8, you'll learn how to how to obtain an Employer Identification Number (EIN) for your loved one's estate and open a bank account in the name of the estate after you have been formally appointed executor. However, your loved one may have bills that are currently due or will be due shortly—before you get an EIN, open the bank account, or contact creditors. Your loved one's immediate bills may include mortgage, rent, utility, insurance, car, tax, and other payments. Your goal is to avoid any activity by a creditor that may result in a loss to the estate by way of repossession, lien, or other negative action. To avoid this situation, you may have to make some immediate payments to creditors. Keep track of these payments so you can be reimbursed from your loved one's estate.

With regard to your loved one's debts, don't pay any debts that don't have to be paid immediately. Debts are required to be paid in the order of their priority and not until the claim period has ended. Failure to pay high-priority debts before low-priority debts may result in the executor becoming personally liable for the debt. In Chapters 9 and 10 you'll learn about contacting your loved one's creditors and paying debts in order of priority after the claim period has ended.

Find Your Loved One's Will and Identify the Executor of the Estate

If you know your loved one has a last will and testament, find it, and identify the executor of your loved one's estate. The executor's identity will be contained in the will and may be referred to as the personal representative. This book uses the terms "executor" and "personal representative" interchangeably. The executor is the person who manages your loved one's estate *after* he or she passes away. The executor is responsible for carrying out the instructions contained in your loved one's will, determining the status of your loved one's finances, paying your loved one's debts, and distributing any remaining assets to his or her heirs. Immediately notify the executor of your loved one's death so he or she can review the will and begin managing your loved one's estate per the terms of the will. Because you're reading this book, you may be the executor. We'll talk more specifically about the will and the executor's role in the next chapter. Now we just need to locate the will, determine the executor, and notify him or her of your love one's passing.

In a perfect world, your loved one has already talked to you (or the executor if you aren't the executor) about his or her will. However, talking about one's own death can be difficult. It wouldn't be surprising if your loved one died without telling family or friends about his or her will. If that's the case, you need to find the will to identify the executor. If your loved one used an attorney in the past, was friends with an attorney, or had some other connection with an attorney, then that's where you begin. If you aren't sure if he or she had an attorney, or who the attorney might be, ask other people close to your loved one for this information. Your loved one's contacts or personal phone book may also reveal his or her attorney's name. Once the attorney is identified, ask if he or she ever drafted a will on your loved one's behalf. If an attorney prepared your loved one's will, he or she will have it on file. The attorney also will be able to identify the executor.

Keep in mind, your loved one may not have hired an attorney to prepare a will. People often write wills on their own. A will prepared by your loved one may be perfectly legally, even if it's handwritten, if it's dated and signed. If your search for an attorney hits a dead end, start looking for a will in your loved one's belongings. I want to make clear that this is a task for the executor, someone who has good reason to believe he or she is the executor, or an immediate family member or next of kin of the loved one.

People typically keep wills in safe places—places they expect someone to look upon their death. Your search should start with your loved one's home. Logical places to search include a home office, study, desk, file box, safe, storage area, or other place where your loved one might keep important documents. Keep in mind that the will may be in electronic form and "filed" in your loved one's computer storage. Your loved one's will may also be in a safe deposit box at his or her bank. Unless you have a joint account with your loved one, or you've been named as an executor or been appointed by the court to act on your loved one's behalf, the bank may not allow you to access his or her safe deposit box. Depending on your relationship with your loved one, the bank will likely require your loved one's death certificate and an order from the court giving you permission to access the safe deposit box.

If you find the will, review it carefully for the name of the executor. Then contact the executor and explain the circumstances. Little explanation will be necessary if your loved one previously informed the executor of his or her role. Even if the executor had no advance warning, he or she likely will assume the role with pride. If not, the will may contain the name of a contingent or backup executor. Otherwise, you may have to petition or formally ask the probate court where your loved one resided at the time of his or her death for assistance in naming an executor.

What If Your Loved One Died Without a Will?

If your loved one died without a will, you'll likely need to apply to the probate court in the county where your loved one resided at the time of death to appoint an executor to manage his or her estate. Depending on your loved one's estate, you may be able to avoid probate. This is discussed in Chapters 6 and 7. Depending on the circumstances, it may take several weeks from the time of your loved one's death until the probate court appoints an executor. In the meantime, continue with the following tasks, as they need to be performed promptly.

Confirm the Cause of Death and Consider the Need for an Autopsy

Before you plan the funeral and have your loved one's body prepared, you need to ensure his or her death was natural. Like many of your other tasks, this may seem unsettling. Intense emotions will be present and shouldn't be ignored. But to perform the tasks your loved one is counting on you to perform, you must approach them in a logical, methodical manner.

In most cases, a loved one's death can be attributed to natural causes such as old age, heart failure, an extended disease, or some other illness. However, on occasion, a death may not be the result of natural causes. Instead, it may be considered a "wrongful" death: a death caused by the willful or negligent act of another. Examples of a wrongful death may include death from a car accident, medical treatment, defective product, manslaughter, murder, or other negligent or intentional act. If your loved one suffered a wrongful death, then his or her beneficiaries may bring a wrongful death civil lawsuit against the party who caused the death. A criminal action against the person who performed the wrongful act also would be likely. Considering its importance, the cause of death needs to be determined before the body is altered.

To determine if the death was natural or the result of a wrongful act, a medical doctor must examine the body. If your loved one passed away in a hospital, its staff will arrange for the attending or treating physician to determine the cause of death. If your loved one passed away at home, in hospice, or in a similar facility, contact your loved one's primary care physician. This doctor will likely determine the cause of death, which will be recorded in a death certificate.

Under certain circumstances you'll need to contact the public coroner of the county where your loved one died. If the death appears wrongful or suspicious in any way, err on the side of caution. Contact the county coroner immediately if your loved one's death occurred under any of the following circumstances:

- The attending doctor at the hospital or your loved one's primary care physician is unable to state the cause of death.
- The death occurred when your loved one was undergoing a medical procedure.
- The death occurred when your loved one was working in his or her employment.
- The death occurred while your loved one was in police custody, a detention center, jail, or prison.
- An accidental death is suspected.
- The death appears suspicious.
- A wrongful death is suspected.
- A suicide is suspected.
- Your loved one is an infant.

If the cause of your loved one's death is uncertain, unknown, or if foul play is suspected, a coroner, pathologist, or other specially trained doctor will perform an autopsy. Some autopsies consist of an external examination of the body, whereas others require an internal examination to determine the cause of death. Depending on the circumstances, an internal autopsy may require the permission of the loved one's next of kin. After the coroner performs the autopsy, he or she will issue a death certificate listing the cause of death. Also, the coroner will contact law enforcement if the death appears wrongful or suspicious.

Once the cause of death has been confirmed, you'll need to arrange to have your loved one's body transferred to a funeral home or other similar facility.

Arrange to Have Your Loved One's Body Transferred
Time permitting, try to make an informed decision as to the

funeral home, crematorium, or other facility you want to handle your loved one's body. Otherwise, you may have to pay to transfer your loved one's body from one facility to another facility. Depending on the size of the community, there may be one or dozens of funeral homes and other such facilities. If you don't have one in mind, ask family and friends for suggestions. The internet and yellow pages also list and review these providers. After you've decided on the funeral home or similar facility, call its director and discuss the body's transfer to the facility, including the cost. The director will ask you for certain information, including the location of your loved one's body and other logistical and personal information. Have your loved one's social security number handy. When you communicate with the funeral home or crematorium, be sure to discuss how to request and obtain death certificates.

Obtain Certified Copies of the Death Certificate

A death certificate is an official document issued by the government that states the date, time, location, cause of death, and other personal information about the deceased. Depending on the state where the death occurred, a family member, legal representative, decedent's doctor, and funeral director may request death certificates from the state. Proof of the requesting party's identity and relationship to the deceased is required. This may include a passport, driver's license, marriage certificate, temporary resident card, or similar identification.

The funeral home should ask you how many certified copies of the death certificate you need. If it doesn't, ask the funeral director for the death certificates. You'll need certified copies of your loved one's death certificate when notifying banks, investment firms, life insurers, the U.S. Department of Veterans Affairs, the Social Security Administration, and others about the death. You'll also need copies when filing your loved one's final tax returns. To determine how many certified copies of the death certificate you'll need, add up your loved one's various accounts to get a rough estimate. Then, ask the funeral home for several more than your rough estimate, as you'll likely need more than you initially thought. Expect to pay between $10 and $20 for each certified death certificate.

If, for some reason, the funeral home can't provide you with the death certificates, then order certified copies from the state in which your loved one passed away. The easiest way to determine how to order the certificates is by searching the internet for the specific state agency that handles this service. You can also order the certified copies through a third-party company by searching the internet for companies that provide the service for a fee.

After the transfer of your loved one's body has been finalized and you've requested certified copies of the death certificate, it's time to take a deep breath and evaluate your own mental and physical health.

Keep Tabs on Your Emotions and Health

There are many beautiful and uplifting things in life, but there's also loss. A loved one's passing is a great loss and one of the most emotional situations you'll ever experience. Losing a loved one will make you question the purpose of life as well as your faith and spirituality. It can trigger intense feelings of grief, which can lead to long-term depression. Keeping tabs on your emotions and taking steps to preserve your mental and physical health is vital. It will also allow you to accomplish the tasks your loved one needs you to complete.

When my mom died, I was overcome with disbelief, fond memories, and regrets. I made a conscious effort to recall all the good times I enjoyed with my mother, but I also recognized how I took our time together for granted, not realizing those times wouldn't last forever. A close friend talked to me about her belief that there are different seasons of our heart and soul, just like there are different seasons on Earth. During our life, our heart and soul will experience all of the seasons. My friend explained to me that it's our responsibility to become self-aware—to embrace the beauty of these seasons and the sorrow. All seasons must run their course. During the season of sorrow, you must pay attention to your own needs more than you ever did before.

Taking care of yourself includes talking about your feelings with your family. Celebrating the joy that your loved one brought you, as well as your regrets, is all a part of healing. The more you do this the better, and the quicker you'll begin the healing process. Do the following to take care of your body, mind, and spirit:

- Eat regularly. Your stomach may be tied in knots, but your body and mind won't function for long without healthy food. Eat regularly, even if you aren't hungry.
- Don't drink too much alcohol. I understand the benefits of a drink, but I also realize the burdens of drinking too much. So do you.
- Exercise regularly. Go for a walk. Ride a bike. Go to the gym. Go fishing. Stimulate your body in whatever way is right for you and feel the emotional benefit.
- Sleep regularly. You have a lot on your mind, but you also need to give your mind and body a break. Try to maintain your regular sleep hours.
- Stay close to your family. If you have family members who are also grieving, it's important to support each other. For me, this was the most important part of taking care of myself.
- Maintain your friendships and welcome gestures of support and comfort. Being around other people can help your attitude and healing. At first, it may be difficult to be with your friends and others. Questions about your loved one, unwanted attention, condolences, and sometimes insensitivity can be tiring. But knowing that other people you care about also care about you can be comforting and help the healing process.
- Keep working. Taking time off work to grieve and to accomplish your tasks as the executor is necessary and recommended. It also gives you much-needed time to heal from the loss. However, you'll likely need to get back

to work to support your lifestyle and family. Getting back to work is also good for your mind and spirit, as it allows you to focus on someone else's problems.

Now that you're keeping tabs on your own mental and physical health, let's reach out to family and friends.

Reach Out to Family and Friends

Reaching out to family and friends is a straightforward task that will keep your momentum going. Family and friends who don't already know of your loved one's death need to get the news of his or her passing directly from you. Obviously, this will be an emotional process for you and your loved one's family and friends. It's also a key part of the healing process.

To start, make a list of everyone you think should know of your loved one's death. The list should include a hierarchy of people your loved one was connected to in any meaningful way. At the top of the list are family members, relatives, and friends. The next tier will be your loved one's employer, co-owners in joint ventures, employees, co-employees, and advisors such as accountants and lawyers. Next include church members, social club acquaintances, tennis buddies, workout partners, and people with this type of connection to your loved one.

At the bottom of the list are creditors, such as credit card companies, and other businesses with which your loved one had some type of financial relationship. These organizations may ask you for information and documents related to his or her death, such as the death certificate. Take note of these requests for future follow-up. In Chapter 8, you'll learn you how to uncover and record your loved one's debts and creditors, and Chapter 9 will discuss how to notify creditors, Social Security, and other pertinent organizations of your loved one's passing. However, if you decide to communicate with these organizations now, ask for all contracts, obligations, deadlines, and outstanding debts related to your loved one.

After you've made the list, determine how to reach out to these people and businesses. The preferred method for telling people close to your loved one is in person or by telephone. This is especially true when it comes to family members, relatives, and friends. If they live close to you, try to speak to them in person. If not, a telephone call is acceptable. It may be easier to send them a text or email, but an in-person meeting or telephone call is necessary under the circumstances. It should go without saying, never leave a voice message to friends or family members stating your loved one has passed. If you call them and get their voicemail, tell them you have urgent news and to please contact you as soon as possible. If you believe it's appropriate to send an email of your loved one's death to a person or organization, make sure your opening sentence warns them that the email brings bad news.

Make sure you consider how the person may react to the news. If the person is ill, fragile, or prone to high emotion, then have another family member or friend present with the person to help comfort them. Try to take as much time as necessary with these people—treat them like your loved one would have liked you to treat them. However, if you have many people to contact, you also need to stay on task. Politely state you can talk again later but have more people to contact now.

Reaching out to family, friends, and others about your loved one's death is emotionally draining and time-consuming. Take your time and realize it may take several days to inform everyone. If you have other close family members who can help with this task, talk to them and explain your strategy for notifying everyone.

Now that you've notified interested persons of your loved one's passing, it's time to write the obituary. Then you'll plan the funeral and have the body prepared.

Write the Obituary

An obituary serves many purposes. It acknowledges the loss of your loved one, shares the joy he or she experienced while on this Earth, and expresses the grief of your loss. In some ways, it's like a mini funeral for those who can't attend the service. It's also a way to remember your loved one in the years to come. The most meaningful obituaries are easy to read, well thought out, and come from the heart.

The first step in writing the obituary is to contact the local newspaper or other publication where you'd like the obituary to appear. Ask for information about the obituary's cost, requirements, and publication date. Many publications have this information online at their websites. Your funeral director can also help you with questions about the obituary.

When writing the obituary, include significant events that happened in your loved one's life, his or her attributes and contributions, and the impact he or she had on family and friends. Include a recent photo with the obituary as a useful way for readers to instantly recognize your loved one. An obituary typically begins with your loved one's name, age, and place of residence, followed by his or her time and place of death. Some people choose to include the cause of death. Sharing the cause of death is a personal decision but may be helpful if the death was sudden, reducing the need to explain it to friends, neighbors, and others.

Next, outline the most important events and qualities of your loved one's life. This is highly personalized but typically includes education, work, military service, hobbies, and organizations with which he or she was associated. You may also want to share something special about your loved one that people may not know. After the biographical sketch, list your loved one's close survivors and those who passed away before him or her. Survivors typically include the spouse, children, grandchildren, parents, and siblings. Take your time and don't forget any close relatives. You may also wish to include the time and place of the service.

Finally, leaving a special message at the end of the obituary allows you to thank people instrumental to your loved one's care. Consider including a poem or motto that meant something special to your loved one, writing a short prayer, or just saying something you want to say. Take your time writing and rewriting the obituary to make sure it's easy to read and includes all key events, contributions, and family members. Review the obituary from the reader's perspective, and make sure it's written with a personal touch that comes from your heart.

You're making good progress toward accomplishing immediate tasks. Now it's time to plan the funeral.

Plan the Funeral

Planning the funeral will involve some creative tasks and working closely with other loved ones and friends. If your loved one put together a funeral plan prior to his or her death, then many of your tasks will be simplified or eliminated. Such a plan likely details the type of service and events your loved one chose for the funeral or memorial service. If no plan exists, it's up to you to plan the service and make some decisions. Keep in mind your loved one's spiritual and religious beliefs and try to envision the type of service he or she would have liked.

The funeral or other service director is a key resource here and will provide you with options, costs, and other specifics related to the funeral or memorial service. This information will be the foundation on which you'll base much of your decision-making. However, it's up to you and your family to finalize the details.

Ask family members their thoughts about the service, and plan the event together. Dividing tasks will make it easier on you and elevate the healing process for all involved. When my mom died, my brothers, sisters, and their spouses gathered for several days around my dad's dining room table to discuss and plan her service and related events. Although my father approved our final plans, he was too grief-stricken to participate in the planning process. This may be the case with someone in your family. If gentle coaxing doesn't work, don't force the person to participate, but keep them in the loop.

My mother had no prior funeral plans, but we had a good idea of what she may have envisioned. Before her medical condition forced her into the hospital, she took time to read spiritual passages related to the end of life. My sisters found a few hand-written poems on my mom's bedside table. They spoke of how a person's image carries on after death and how my mom wanted to be remembered. Not only did the poems reveal that my mom had come to terms with her own mortality and decided to die in a noble, positive way, they also guided our decision-making for her service.

I encourage you to gather family and loved ones around your own dining room table, enjoy each other's comfort, and discover little things about your loved one you never knew. Later on, you may realize you never felt closer to your family than this time when you planned your loved one's service. Involving others in the planning process is therapeutic and quickly accomplishes the tasks that need to be done. Now, let's discuss some funeral choices.

The "Traditional" Funeral

Many traditional funerals involve some combination of a funeral service at a church, crematorium, graveside, funeral home or other place, the burial or cremation, and a memorial service afterward. Funerals may also include other events, such as a viewing or visitation before the funeral and a reception or gathering after the funeral or memorial service. Knowledge of your loved one's personality and spiritual beliefs will give you a good idea of what type of service is appropriate.

After you decide on the appropriate service, take some time to research where you want it to be held. Then contact the church or other facility to arrange the service and check availability. You may decide to reserve a specific date, but don't book the facility until you've confirmed the availability of other loved ones for that date.

The next step is to determine who you'll invite to the service. The selection process will be similar to the process you went through when deciding who to notify about your loved one's death. Try to think about the people your loved one would want to attend, not necessarily who you want to attend. Try to verify when family members and other loved ones are available, but don't try to coordinate everyone's schedule. Then call the facility, book the date, finalize any related paperwork, and notify family and friends.

If the service calls for family and friends to participate in the service, speak with them about what you would like them to do. Typical tasks include officiating the funeral or memorial service; serving as a pallbearer; delivering a eulogy; reading prayers, poems, or other readings; and singing and playing songs and hymns. Be creative and let your loved one's beliefs and family circumstances guide your choices.

My family held two small services for my mother because she maintained close ties to Pennsylvania, her birth state, and New Jersey, the state where she lived when she died. The first service was held in New Jersey after my mom's body was cremated. The second service took place a few weeks later in Pennsylvania. My siblings and I read inspirational and religious passages and told family stories (and a few secrets) about my mom. We kept it lighthearted and positive, per the message of my mom's poems, and encouraged friends in attendance to tell their own stories. One of my parents' "adopted" grandsons wrote and read a lively poem about how he imagined my mom and dad acting on a date in their younger days. He brought the crowd to joyful tears. I encourage you to treat this as a celebration of your loved one's life and involve family members and friends in the ceremony.

Funeral and Cremation Expenses

Funeral expenses vary widely, depending on the part of the country where the funeral will be held. You can expect to pay between $8,000 and $12,000 for a traditional funeral in the United States. This price includes the funeral director's fee, the cost of a casket, embalming, use of the funeral home for the funeral service, the cost of the grave site, the cost to dig the grave, the cost of a grave liner or outer burial container, and the cost of a headstone. Review whether your loved one has insurance to cover funeral expenses or paid the costs in advance.

Although a traditional funeral is still the most popular way to care for the deceased, cremation is quickly gaining in popularity. Like funeral expenses, the cost of a cremation varies widely. A cremation without any additional services may cost less than $1,000. However, you can expect to pay much more for a cremation if it's purchased through a funeral home, especially if the funeral home doesn't have its own crematorium and relies on a third party for the service. You can also "bundle" typical funeral amenities with the cremation, which raises the service's price. For example, you may choose to add a cremation casket, embalming services, use of the funeral home for a service, flowers, and other amenities.

With few exceptions funeral homes and crematoriums aren't required to post their rates in print or online. To compare prices, you need to call or visit the funeral home. Although many people choose to believe that services performed by funeral homes don't vary widely, statistics show this isn't true. I recommend calling or visiting several funeral homes or crematoriums and comparing their services and costs. Only then will you feel comfortable with these final arrangements.

The "Green" Funeral Option

A green funeral, or "natural burial," is an alternative to a traditional funeral, which involves embalming, vaults, liners, and other "toxic" methods used to slow the body's decomposition. With a green funeral, the loved one's body is cared for in a way that attempts to reduce any environmental impact. It typically involves preparing the body without embalming fluid or chemical preservatives. The body may be wrapped in a shroud or placed in a biodegradable coffin or casket. It's then buried in a shallow grave, either on private land or in a cemetery that allows for this vault-free technique. Natural burials have been practiced all over the world for thousands of years. Some religions forbid anything other than natural burials and consider embalming or other procedures designed to preserve the body as desecration. Green burial cemeteries exist in several states, although many counties regulate green burials.

In most cases, the cost of a green funeral is much less than the cost of a tradition funeral or cremation. This is because expenses related to embalming, decay-resistant caskets or coffins, vaults, funeral home services, limousines, and other traditional costs are avoided with a green funeral. However, the cost of a green burial will increase if the body is buried on land that's preserved in perpetuity with ongoing preservation. If you're interested in learning more about green burials, the Green Burial Counsel (www.greenburial.org) is a nonprofit organization that established the country's first certifiable standards for green burials, and many conventional funeral providers offer a burial package certified by this counsel.

Chapter Summary

This chapter took us through the immediate tasks that needed to be done after your loved one passed away, ranging from finding the will to planning the funeral. You likely encountered more than one setback along the way, which is to be expected. Take a moment to look back on all the difficult tasks you accomplished and keep visualizing the goal of settling your loved one's estate. This will keep you motivated. Stay positive, and remember you aren't in this alone.

The next chapter will move quickly as you learn how to decipher the will, understand the executor's role, and determine your loved one's beneficiaries.

Chapter 5

Deciphering the Will, Understanding the Executor's Role, and Determining Beneficiaries

Congratulations! You've already accomplished a lot and built momentum. In this chapter, you'll learn how to decipher the will, understand the executor's role, and determine your loved one's beneficiaries. Use the streamlined definitions in the Glossary at the back of this book as a reference while you move through the process of settling your loved one's estate. Many of the terms you'll read or hear are uncommon and may sound complicated. Legally, they have a specific meaning that a professional, such as a lawyer, understands. Don't let these words intimidate you. Be familiar with their basic meanings and refer back to their definitions when needed. Your familiarity with the terms will help you accomplish your duties with confidence.

Overview of a Will

The will is the crucial document that applies *after* your loved one has passed away. It contains your loved one's final requests and describes how he or she wants real and personal property to be distributed. The will must be filed with the probate court, but not everyone has a will at the time of their death. If your loved one doesn't have a will, the law of the state in which he or she resided at the time of death will detail how the estate will be divided after creditors have been paid. This situation is discussed in Chapter 6. Like the living will, your loved had to be of sound mind when he or she signed the will for it to be valid. The executor is the key person related to the will.

The Executor's Role and Duties

In the will, your loved one would have designated an executor to carry out the instructions contained in the will and to finalize details related to the property owned at the time of death. You identified the executor in Chapter 4 and notified him or her of your loved one's passing. Although this book predominantly uses the term "executor" to refer to the person appointed by the will to carry out your loved one's requests after his or her death, this person also may be known and referred to as the "personal representative."

The executor is legally responsible for determining the status of your loved one's financial situation, paying debts, including taxes, and distributing any remaining assets to the heirs. In essence, the executor manages your loved one's estate. The executor has a legal duty to act with honesty, impartiality, and care in performing his or her duties. An executor must be flexible and capable of performing different tasks in a timely manner until they are completed. An executor also may be required to appear in court on behalf of the estate.

If you, as the executor, don't understand the terms of the will or find the probate process to be beyond your capabilities, don't hesitate to seek legal advice from a competent probate attorney to ensure you're complying with your duties. The executor may be personally liable to the loved one's estate or beneficiaries if he or she doesn't perform the duties correctly and the estate or beneficiaries are consequently damaged. Your loved one's estate typically will incur the cost of the probate attorney. Often, the best way to find a competent probate attorney is through word of mouth, such as a recommendation from a trusted family member or friend. The county or state bar associations where your loved one resided is also a good source for obtaining a recommendation.

Depending on the size and complexity of your loved one's estate, your job as the executor may be relatively easy or more challenging. Either way, expect to experience some level of stress due to the responsibilities involved, timeline for getting tasks done, and your likely unfamiliarity with the required tasks. Being organized is a key to your success, so set up a separate filing system for the estate, and keep copies of everything you have sent and received from creditors, beneficiaries, financial institutions, and anyone else. With a little organization and careful record keeping, an executor's obligations don't have to be overwhelming.

A certain amount of endurance and pace is required on the executor's part, as the probate process typically takes between six months and two years from the opening of the estate until its closing. Try not to let that overwhelm you, as many of those days will be spent waiting on the probate court.

Finally, you may want to please everyone by settling your loved one's estate quickly. Resist the urge to rush the process, as it may cause you to miss a crucial step. Relax, take a deep breath, and keep moving forward. Always keep your loved one in mind. You're doing this as one of your last selfless acts on your loved one's behalf. With these thoughts guiding your mindset and actions, you're sure to succeed.

The Executor's Compensation

An executor is usually entitled to payment for his or her services, with the payment coming from the loved one's estate. If your loved one's will doesn't address the executor's compensation, then the law in the state in which you're opening your loved one's probate estate will govern if and how the executor is paid. Payment may equal a percentage of the estate, a flat fee, or an hourly rate approved by the probate court. A simple internet search should reveal the process in your state. Narrow your search to the local probate court, which typically will have a website with useful information and answers to frequently asked questions.

It isn't uncommon for a family member acting as the executor to decline payment. He or she may consider it an honor to be chosen to carry out the loved one's final requests. Whether or not you decide to accept payment is a personal decision to be made by you alone. Everyone's situation is different. Consider the time you put into performing your duties as the executor, your financial situation, whether you lost time and compensation from employment while performing your duties as the executor, the effect of your decision on your loved one's heirs if you decide to accept payment, and other factors you think are applicable to your situation.

Note that any compensation you earn performing your duties as executor is treated as income, which you need to declare as income on your tax returns. Because executor compensation is taxable, and inheritances are generally not taxable, it may be financially beneficial to decline any fees. If you, the executor, are going to inherit a large portion of the estate you may end up with more after-tax value if you decline compensation. Payment of the executor's compensation by the estate may take priority over paying many other debts. This topic is covered in more detail in Chapter 10.

Now that you have a working knowledge of the will and the executor's role, it's time to review the will and determine your loved one's assets, beneficiaries, debts, and creditors.

Review and Understand the Will

As executor, you need to thoroughly read the will and any codicil or amendment to the will. As stated in the Glossary, a codicil is simply a document that changes the existing will in some way. It's typically used to make fairly minor changes without drafting a new will. For instance, a codicil may be used to change the executor, add a new asset, or change a beneficiary. Thoroughly familiarize yourself with the will's contents and any codicil.

Your initial reading of the will will give you a basic understanding of your loved one's wishes, who will inherit the property, and generally what your loved one wants you to accomplish. Read the will several times to ensure you're confident that you understand its contents. I suggest you make a personal copy of the will, highlight the document, and take notes as you see fit. After you understand the will's contents, it's time to move forward with the nuts and bolts of administering the estate.

Determine Your Loved One's Beneficiaries

As you know, a beneficiary is a person named by your loved one in his or her will to receive specific property. A beneficiary is sometimes called an "heir." Your review of the will has identified your loved one's beneficiaries and what they are entitled to receive under the will. It's likely that the will will also state the percentage of the estate each heir is entitled to receive after all debts have been paid and specific assets or bequests have been distributed. This is called the heirs' "residuary percentage." Related to residuary percentage is "residuary estate," which is the remaining value of the estate after all debts have been paid and any specific bequests have been distributed. For example, if the will states that a particular heir is entitled to 50 percent of the residuary estate, his or her residuary percentage is 50 precent of the remaining value of the estate after all debts have been paid and any specific bequests have been distributed. If the residuary estate is worth $100,000, then the heir is entitled to receive $50,000 in cash and assets.

Stay organized by recording each beneficiary's name, the asset the beneficiary is entitled to receive, the asset's value, and whether the asset is subject to a lien. An Inventory List is contained in the Appendix. It's a good practice to use the Appendix's Inventory List, Debt Form, and Executor's Checklist to record important information as it's uncovered and to stay on track.

Evaluate the Need for Professional Help

Now that you've reviewed the will, you should have a clearer idea of the size of your loved one's estate and how complicated it might be to administer it. Depending on the circumstances and your personality and abilities, you should consider speaking with professionals who can assist you. An attorney familiar with your situation and the probate laws in your area can advise you on specific legal steps based on your situation. Likewise, an accountant can assist you with providing a final accounting to the probate court and closing the estate. These advisors can be your liaison with the probate court, creditors, beneficiaries, and others. Even if you don't think you need to discuss the matter with a professional at this time, keep the option open as you work your way through the probate process. Although I wrote this book to help guide you through the process, your specific circumstances may dictate a need for professional help.

In the next chapter, I'll tell you what you need to know about probate, what property is subject to probate, how to determine if you need probate, whether you can avoid probate, and how to determine the probate process in your state. Maintain your momentum and move on!

Chapter 6

What You Need to Know About Probate

I n this chapter, you'll learn what you need to know about probate. This includes an overview of probate, what property is and isn't subject to probate, how to evaluate the need for probate, and how to determine the probate process in your state. In the next chapter, you'll learn when, where, and how to open probate.

To some, the tasks you'll perform in this chapter and the next chapter will be the most challenging part of your journey, simply because the probate process is involved. Although probate may sound lawyerly and intimidating, don't let your preconceptions or fear of the unknown deter you from accomplishing what your loved one knew you could accomplish. After all, probate is simply the process of reviewing the will and administering your loved one's estate according to the terms of the will. Forget about being intimidated and instead learn what you need to know about probate.

Probate Overview

In a nutshell, probate is the court-supervised process to wrap up the affairs of the deceased. It involves appointing an executor, reviewing the will (if there is one), determining whether the will is legal, and administering the estate according to the terms of the will.

The probate process includes determining your loved one's assets, debts, heirs, and creditors; notifying creditors of your loved one's death; and giving creditors the opportunity to request payment of those debts. The executor then pays the loved one's legitimate debts and distributes the remaining assets to the heirs. If your loved one died without a will, the court will appoint an "administrator" to administer the estate according to applicable law.

With a few exceptions, the probate process takes place in the probate court where your loved one resided at the time of his or her death. It begins when the petition for probate and appointment of executor is filed with the court. Some locations refer to this as "opening an estate." With the probate court's oversight, assistance, and approval, an executor will be assigned, your loved one's debts will be paid, and the remaining assets will be distributed to the heirs. Probate closes after an itemized final accounting of your loved one's estate and financial activities is approved by the probate court. Because the probate process gives the executor the legal authority to administer the assets, you must apply for probate when it's needed so the executor can obtain authority from the court to assess and transfer your loved one's assets to the heirs.

Your loved one's estate may be subject to probate whether or not he or she died with a will. We'll discuss the probate process in both situations. Your basic understanding of the probate process will allow you to move forward and accomplish the step-by-step tasks involved in what's often referred to as "opening probate" for your loved one's estate.

When Your Loved One Has a Will

If your loved one had a will when he or she passed away, the probate court will supervise your loved one's probate estate. This includes confirming that the will is valid and ensuring that your loved one's property is disposed of properly, the debts are paid, and the remaining assets are distributed to the heirs per the terms of the will. When these tasks are accomplished, the probate court will close your loved one's probate estate.

In rare cases, a person may contest the validity of the will. For your loved one's will to be valid, he or she must have been of sound mind when the will was executed and intended to dispose of the property as written in the will. In contested matters, the probate court will "authenticate" the will and determine its validity. After the court authenticates the will, it will decide who will receive the loved one's property and in what amount per the terms of the will.

When Your Loved One Doesn't Have a Will

If your loved one passed away without a will, he or she is said to have died "intestate" (without a will). In this situation, the probate court will appoint an administrator to administer the estate according to the applicable law. It's likely that the probate court will also appoint an executor or personal representative to manage, control, and direct your loved one's estate. Considering there is no will, the probate court will also decide how your loved one's estate will be distributed. The intestacy laws of the state where your loved one resided at the time of death outline the system for determining your loved one's heirs and how much property they are entitled to inherit.

Generally, your loved one's heirs will inherit property depending on their degree of kinship. For example, your loved one's spouse and children have the closest degree of kinship and will be first in line to inherit his or her property. If your loved one passed away without a spouse or any living children, then his or her other living descendants would inherit the property. Descendants are people in the blood stream of the ancestor. In addition to any children, descendants may include your loved one's brothers, sisters, grandchildren, and great grandchildren. If there are no living descendants, your loved one's ascendants would inherit the property. Ascendants include grandparents, great grandparents, great aunts, great uncles, and so forth up the family tree.

What Property Isn't Subject to Probate?

Not all of your loved one's property will be subject to probate or the probate court's oversight. Some of your loved one's property will pass automatically upon his or her death. Property owned by your loved one that includes a named beneficiary or joint account holder isn't subject to probate. Examples of beneficiary accounts include bank accounts, retirement accounts, and insurance policies that name a person as a beneficiary. The proceeds of these accounts or policies that name a beneficiary will pass automatically to the beneficiary upon the loved one's death without the need for probate.

Also, property that your loved one holds in "joint tenancy" with another person will automatically pass to the other person (the joint tenant) without the need for probate when your loved one passes away. A home is an example of property commonly held in joint tenancy. In addition, assets that your loved one placed into a trust typically don't need to go through the probate process and can be disbursed immediately without court approval per the terms of the trust. Household goods and other personal property that go to immediate family members will automatically pass to the family members depending on your state's law.

How to Avoid Probate

As previously mentioned, property held by your loved one in joint tenancy, property that includes a named beneficiary, property held in a trust, and certain property per state law typically isn't subject to probate. Likewise, you may be able to avoid probate and not have to file a petition for probate if your loved one's estate is "small." Small estates are those in which the loved one's personal property is worth less than a certain amount, and there is no real estate to transfer. This amount is often referred to as the "threshold amount." The specific threshold amount is determined by the law of the state where your loved one resided at the time of death (the place where the estate would likely be subject to probate). For example, at the time of this writing, the threshold amount is $50,000 for a small estate in New York, $75,000 in Texas, $100,000 in Arizona, and $166,250 in California. The internet will tell you the threshold amount in your loved one's state, but verify the amount with the probate court.

If your loved one's estate is valued at less than the threshold amount, and there is no real estate to transfer, then you typically can avoid filing a petition for probate. Instead, you will just have to complete and sign an affidavit under oath stating the name of your loved one's successors, that the total fair market value of your loved one's personal property is less than the threshold amount, and the successors are entitled to your loved one's personal property.

Check to see if the probate court in the county where your loved resided at the time of his or her death provides sample affidavits for you to complete and any other documents that may be required to support the affidavit, such as the death certificate. Depending on the state, this affidavit may be called a "small estate affidavit" or a similar name. Most courts have sample, fill-in-the-blank forms and affidavits, along with instructions for completing the required forms. You can access them at the local courthouse or on the court's website.

You, or any of your loved one's heirs or successors, would then present the affidavit and other supporting documents, such as the death certificate, to the person or business holding your loved one's assets and request those assets. For example, you may show the affidavit and death certificate to the bank where your loved one has a checking and savings account and request the money be transferred to you or your loved one's successors. You, or the heir collecting the money or other asset, would then be responsible for distributing it to the other heirs per state law. If the person or business holding your loved one's personal property refuses to honor the affidavit, they may be liable for your costs and attorney fees spent hiring a lawyer to enforce the affidavit. The affidavit must be of the proper form, signed, and notarized per the requirements of the applicable state.

The following is a more detailed scenario in which the deceased's estate is under the threshold amount set by state law:

Ann died in Colorado in 2018. Her estate was valued at $66,000. Ann didn't own any real property (real estate). Ann's estate is considered a small estate under Colorado law because it's valued at less than the $70,000 threshold amount set by the state, and she has no real estate to transfer. Ann was survived by two daughters, Diane and Laurie, her successors. Of the $66,000 in Ann's estate, $30,000 was in Ann's personal bank account. Diane completed a form called "Affidavit for the Collection of Personal Property of a Decedent" and signed it before a notary public. Diane presented the signed and notarized affidavit, along with a certified copy of Ann's death certificate, to the bank where Ann had the $30,000 bank account. Diane withdrew the $30,000, distributed $15,000 to Laurie, and kept the remaining $15,000.

Because Ann died with an estate valued at less than the threshold amount set by the law of the state where Ann resided at the time of her death, and there was no real estate to be transferred, Diane was able to withdraw the money from Ann's account by presenting the affidavit and death certificate to Ann's bank. Diane was then responsible for distributing one half of the proceeds to her sister Laurie per state law. So long as Diane presented the bank with the proper information per state law (the affidavit and certified death certificate), the bank was required to allow Diane to withdraw the money from Ann's bank account.

The Probate Process in Your Loved One's State and Probate Forms

To determine whether or not your loved one's estate may avoid probate, you need to review the probate process in the state where your loved one resided at the time of his or her death. With a little time, patience, and persistence, you can accomplish this task. The internet contains a wide range of general information regarding probate and can greatly assist with your review. However, when you need information specific to probate and your loved one's estate, contact the local probate court.

Local probate courts are usually sympathetic and receptive to questions about the probate process in their state. Most states have court or "judicial branch" websites that provide probate information, probate instructions, and forms. In addition, although court personnel aren't permitted to provide you with legal advice, a clerk or self-help assistant at the probate court may be able to help you with more specific questions that aren't addressed on the probate court's website. Consider the probate court and associated website as primary resources in determining the probate process in your state and whether or not your loved one's estate may be able to avoid probate. Always be respectful and patient with the probate court's personnel. They are usually hardworking, underpaid government employees who know the probate judges and will be happy to help you.

Chapter Summary

In this chapter, you learned what you need to know about the probate process, what property and estates may not be subject to probate, and how to use your local probate court to your advantage. In the next chapter, you'll learn how to open the estate. Stay focused, and use your momentum to move through what likely will be more unfamiliar ground. With confidence, we'll work through a series of logical steps to open your loved one's estate, appoint the executor, and authenticate the will. Let's get it done!

Chapter 7

Opening the Estate and Probate

I n this chapter, you'll learn how to open your loved one's estate, often referred to as "opening probate." This includes filing the petition to open probate, receiving appointment as executor, and authenticating the will. To get to this stage, you have done a lot of maneuvering and more than your fair share of mental and physical lifting. Stay focused, and let's keep the momentum going!

When, Where, and How to "Open" Probate

As you'll see, opening probate is a logical process that involves reviewing your particular circumstances to determine when, where, and how to open probate.

When to Open Probate

Depending on the state where you intend to open probate, there will be a deadline to file the petition to open probate. The deadline begins to run immediately upon the date of your loved one's death and may require probate to be opened as soon as 30 days after the death. Some states are more lenient and permit up to several years to open probate. Determine the deadline to open probate in your state and make sure you do so, if needed, before the deadline.

Your state may also have a required waiting period before you can open probate. For example, in some states you must wait 120 hours (five days) after your loved one's death before you can open probate. An internet search of your applicable probate court will reveal any required waiting period.

Where to Open Probate

You'll open probate in the probate court in the county where your loved one resided at the time of death. If your loved one owned real property in a state other than the state where he or she resided at the time of death, then you may be able to open probate in that other state. This may give you more than one choice where to open probate —either in the county where your loved one resided at death or the county in the state where your loved one owned real property. Depending on the situation, it may be more convenient for you, as the executor, to open the estate in the county and state where your loved one owned real property but didn't reside at the time of death. Otherwise, plan on opening probate in the probate court in the county in which your loved one resided at the time of death.

How to Open Probate

You'll open probate by filing the necessary paperwork, which depends on the type of probate you plan to open. Such paperwork will likely include a petition for probate, appointment of the executor, and the will (if any). The probate court often has forms for the petition for probate and appointment of executor for you to complete. Once completed, you file the documents (sometimes called "pleadings") with the clerk's office at the applicable probate court and pay a filing fee. The clerk will then open your loved one's probate estate, assign a corresponding case or matter number, and assign the case to a probate judge or probate registrar to oversee the matter. The court may waive the filing fee if you can show a hardship condition.

Now that you've determined the basics of when, where, and how to open probate for your loved one's estate, you'll determine whether to open formal or informal probate.

Determine Whether to Open a Formal or Informal Estate

Many states give you the option of opening either a formal or an informal estate, which may be called "formal" or "informal" probate. Informal probate is often referred to as "simple probate" or "summary administration." You can expect informal probate to be overseen by a probate registrar. A probate court judge will oversee a formal probate matter. Again, be aware of any deadlines your state may have for opening probate. An overview of informal and formal probate, as well as their pros and cons, will help you determine whether to open the estate formally or informally.

Informal Probate

As its name indicates, informal probate is less formal, more streamlined, less time-consuming, and usually less costly than formal probate. Informal probate is a good option when the heirs agree about the estate and the executor, the assets and debts are straightforward, and you don't anticipate any creditor or other problems. To be eligible for informal probate, most states require the value of the estate to be below a certain dollar amount, called a "threshold amount." Like the threshold amount discussed with the "small" estate in Chapter 6, threshold amounts vary greatly from state to state. Expect the threshold to range from $50,000 to $200,000, depending on the state. Perform an internet search for the probate court where you intend to open probate to determine your state's threshold amount.

Presuming that your loved one's estate appears straightforward— no disagreements among heirs and no issues with assets and liabilities —you now need to determine whether the value of your loved one's estate falls under the threshold amount and may qualify for informal probate. Simply put, the value of the estate is calculated by deter- mining your loved one's assets (value of real and personal property) and liabilities (amount of debts) and subtracting the liabilities from the assets. The resulting amount will give you the approximate value of your loved one's estate. You may also have a reasonable idea of the estate's value from your review of the will (Chapter 5) and your loved one's circumstances. Even if your loved one passed away without a will, you may know the approximate value of the estate so you can determine if it falls under the threshold amount.

If you're unable to come up with an approximate value of the estate at this time, you'll need to dig deeper to value the estate and determine if it qualifies for informal probate. Chapter 8 details how to value your loved one's estate. Make sure you give yourself enough time after valuing the estate to meet the deadline to open probate.

Formal Probate

Formal probate is overseen by a probate court judge. It provides an extra layer of security with court oversight in administering and closing the estate. Formal probate is recommended when the heirs aren't in agreement regarding the will or appointing an executor, your loved one's assets and debts are complicated or in dispute, or the estate is large and more complex. Formal probate proceedings are more time-consuming and expensive. If you think formal probate is needed to settle your loved one's estate, and the issues are outside your knowledge or comfort zone, you shouldn't hesitate to consult an attorney.

Take some time to analyze the circumstances of your loved one's estate and anticipate possible issues that may arise during the probate process. This reflection should guide you toward choosing either informal or formal probate. Although most people prefer a stream-lined, less formal process, it's more important to logically determine whether informal or formal probate is the best option for your loved one's estate. If you file for informal probate, the probate registrar may determine that your loved one's estate doesn't fit the informal probate process. In that case, you'll be required to open formal probate.

Open Probate

Now that you've reviewed and analyzed the circumstances of your loved one's estate and determined whether to use informal or formal probate, it's time to open probate. Whether you open informal or formal probate, you'll be required to perform certain tasks in an orderly fashion pursuant to a timeline set by the probate court. These tasks depend on your state's probate court, but they typically include

(1) completing the necessary paperwork, such as the application or petition for probate and appointment of the executor; (2) filing the necessary paperwork with the probate court; (3) obtaining an initial hearing date with the probate court if you picked formal probate; (4) providing notice of the hearing to interested people; (5) preparing for the initial hearing; and (6) attending the initial hearing, in which the executor will be appointed and the will likely will be validated (if there is a will).

Complete the Necessary Paperwork

The necessary paperwork involved with opening an estate varies, depending on the state and county where the probate court is located, the type of estate you're opening, and whether your loved one died with or without a will. As a rule of thumb, opening a formal estate involves more paperwork than opening an informal estate. All necessary paperwork is filed with the clerk of the probate court in the county where you are filing probate.

My website, https://www.georgekoons.com/subscribe, contains numerous sample court forms, often called "pleadings," that may be used in a typical probate case. You can access these pleadings by subscribing to my newsletter. These court pleadings are provided to give you an idea of the information that a typical form or pleading may include in its contents. They shouldn't be relied on for your matter because they aren't specific to your loved one's estate or situation. Contact the probate court in the county where you intend to open probate for preprinted, fill-in-the-blank forms required for opening an informal or formal estate, appointing an executor, and other related matters. Many courts provide these forms, as well as instructions for completing them, for free. One or more of these forms will reference your will, which should be attached to the form as directed.

Consider your local probate court as your go-to resource. As your probate matter progresses through the system, you can contact the probate court clerk regarding the status of your case, documents that have been filed, and other matters. You'll need to reference your case number, which the filing clerk will give you when you file your initial documents opening probate.

Informal Probate. If you decided to file informal probate, the required paperwork will likely include an application provided by the probate court for informal probate and appointment of an executor or personal representative. This application will require you to provide specific information regarding yourself as the applicant; your loved one; his or her death; any will; your loved one's spouse, children, and other heirs; your nomination as the executor; and other information. Applications and forms provided by the probate court are easy to read, understand, and fill out. The probate court is also familiar with their format.

Other paperwork may include your acceptance and agreement to perform the duties of executor as well as a proposed order for the probate registrar to sign ordering informal probate and appointing your loved one's executor. Pay attention to any attachments required by the paperwork. For instance, the form may direct you to include the death certificate, original will, or other document with the form. If your loved one died without a will, or if the will doesn't appoint an executor, then the probate registrar will appoint an administrator. Typically, the probate registrar will review the paperwork without requiring a formal hearing.

Formal Probate. If you chose to open formal probate, most states require you to file a petition for formal probate of the will and formal appointment of the executor. Basically, a petition gets the case started; it's simply the name of a document filed with the court requesting the court act on a matter. The petition will include information related to the person filing the petition; your loved one; his or her death; the will; your loved one's spouse, children, and other heirs; the person nominated as executor; compensation of the executor; administration of the estate; and related information. Typically, the petition will direct that the death certificate and original will be included with the petition.

Depending on your state, other necessary paperwork may

include your acceptance and agreement to perform the duties of executor; a notice of a hearing on the petition for formal probate and formal appointment of the executor, stating the time and place of the hearing; a proposed order for the judge to sign permitting the will to formal probate and formally appointing the executor; and other related documents.

Forms related to the required paperwork, and instructions for completing the forms, may be found at the specific probate court or on its website. A probate court judge reviews the paperwork in a formal probate process and likely will require a hearing on the petition for formal probate of the will and formal appointment of the executor.

When Your Loved One Died Without a Will. If your loved one passed away <u>without</u> a will, he or she is said to have died "intestate." To open informal or formal probate when your loved one died without a will, the required paperwork will likely include a document called a "petition for adjudication of intestacy and formal appointment of a personal representative" or something similar. In simpler terms, this document requests the probate court (1) open a probate matter related to your loved one's estate; (2) appoint a personal representative (similar to an executor) to manage, control, and direct your loved one's estate, and (3) decide how your loved one's estate will be distributed per the state's intestacy laws.

The petition for adjudication of intestacy and formal appointment of a personal representative will include information related to the person filing the petition; your loved one; your loved one's spouse, children, and other heirs; the person nominated as your loved one's personal representative; compensation of the personal representative; how the estate is to be administered; and other information. It must be signed under oath and notarized.

Depending on your state, other necessary paperwork may include your acceptance and agreement to perform the duties of a personal representative, a notice of a hearing on the petition stating the time and place of the hearing, and a proposed order for the judge to sign determining your loved one's heirs and appointing the personal representative. Forms related to the required paperwork, and instructions for completing the forms, may be found at the specific probate court or on its website.

Depending on your loved one's estate and your background, attention to detail, and willingness to spend some time with the probate process, you may feel confident in your ability to open the formal estate and proceed through the process of settling the estate. However, if after speaking with the probate court and reviewing the required forms you think you are in over your head, then you should contact a probate attorney for advice.

File the Paperwork with the Probate Court

After you've filled out the required paperwork and gathered the required attachments, such as the death certificate and original will, you'll need to file the paperwork. This is done by taking it to the probate clerk at the courthouse in the county where you intend to open your loved one's estate and asking the clerk to file it. You will have to pay a court filing fee unless you can't afford the filing fee. In that case, you'll need to complete a form requesting a waiver of the filing fee. Once the case is filed, the clerk will provide you with a case number related to your probate case. You'll reference this case number, which identifies your specific probate matter, when communicating with the court.

Obtain an Initial Hearing Date (Formal Probate)

If you've chosen to file formal probate, you'll need to get a hearing date from the court clerk on your petition for formal probate of the will and formal appointment of the executor. For clarity, let's refer to this as the "initial hearing." Depending on the probate court, the judge may also determine the validity of the will at the initial hearing. The probate court clerk will schedule the initial hearing date when you file your petition. The purpose of the hearing is to give interested parties a chance to object to the appointment of the executor and the validity of the will. A hearing usually isn't required if you filed informal probate.

Provide Interested People Notice of the Initial Hearing (Formal Probate)

Once you obtain the initial hearing date, you must give interested people written notice of the date, time, location, and substance of the hearing. Interested people are those who can inherit something from your loved one's estate. They include your loved one's spouse, children, siblings, and other heirs. This written notice is usually referred to as a "Notice of Hearing" and is likely one of the forms that the probate court has for your use. You just need to fill out the form, providing the date, time, location, and purpose of the hearing (that you have filed a petition for formal probate of the will and formal appointment of the executor). Include a copy of the petition for formal probate of the will and formal appointment of the executor with the notice as directed. Then send the notice to the interested people via first-class U.S. Mail.

Out of an abundance of caution, you may want to send notices and other documents to interested people via first-class U.S. Mail return receipt requested. Although it's more costly and time-consuming, it provides confirmation and evidence that the person received the notice. Keep all related receipts and postal confirmations.

Prepare for the Initial Hearing (Formal Probate)

You always want to take as much time as you need to prepare for any hearing with the court. Preparation means reviewing and knowing the contents of your file, paperwork, pleadings filed with the court, the will, and other documents related to your loved one's estate. You don't need to memorize the contents of the file, such as each reference in the will. However, you should be able to quickly access the information or document as needed.

Organizing the documents in a notebook or folder with heading tabs will allow you to quickly reference the information. Your review of the file should be straightforward, considering all the information and knowledge you have gained thus far regarding your loved one's estate. Take note of any potential issues or concerns you're aware of that may arise at the hearing. You may want to write these issues down in bullet-point fashion to keep your thoughts concise, orga-nized, and easy to reference. Your preparation and knowledge of the background, intricacies, and possible issues with your loved one's estate will give you confidence and instill confidence in the court when the judge speaks to you. Until you're in the initial hearing, you really don't know what questions the court may ask of you. Thorough preparation is the key to a smooth hearing.

Attend the Initial Hearing (Formal Probate)

On the date of the hearing, arrive at the courthouse a little before your hearing time so you can familiarize yourself with the layout of the courthouse and locate the specific courtroom where your hearing will be held. Of course, dress neatly, preferably in business or busi-ness casual attire. Silence your cell phone and other devices and check in with the judge's clerk in the specific courtroom where your matter is assigned.

The judge or the judge's assistant will call your case number and ask you to introduce yourself. A typical interaction with the judge involves speaking when spoken to and responding specifically to the judge's questions. Most courts are backlogged with cases and have a packed schedule. The judge will appreciate you focusing your answers on his or her specific questions. Addressing the judge as "Your Honor" is proper protocol and shows respect for the judge and the legal process. Having said this, the judge and his staff recognize that you are appearing on behalf of your loved one's estate and without an attorney. This is referred to as appearing "pro se" or "pro per." As such, they will be lenient with you and not hold you to the standard of an attorney. Nonetheless, the court will appreciate your thorough preparation and appropriate conduct.

Appointing the Executor, Posting Bond, and Addressing Immediate Concerns. Most of the time no one objects to the executor's appointment. Typically, courts will honor the loved one's wishes and appoint the executor that was named in the will. If there is no will, state law determines who has priority to serve as executor. Understand that the court is required to hold the

initial hearing on the petition and appointment of executor as part of its procedure, so try not to be anxious.

Once the executor is approved by the probate judge, the court will issue certified documents opening probate and allowing the executor to act on behalf of the loved one's estate. These documents are typically called "Letters of Administration" or "Letters Testamentary" if there is no will. These are legal documents showing you, as executor, are the person in charge of your loved one's estate. You will also sign this or another document legally agreeing to act as executor and to oversee matters involving the estate. Depending on state requirements, you may also have to post bond. A bond is an insurance policy that protects beneficiaries of the will in the event the executor intentionally or unintentionally makes a costly error during the probate process. If a bond is required, the amount will depend on the size of your loved one's estate. However, if the will states that no bond is required, the court will often waive the requirement.

You may have immediate concerns or issues you want to discuss with the probate judge at the initial hearing. For instance, your loved one may have had bills that needed to be paid immediately. These bills may have included mortgage, rent, utility, insurance, car, tax, and other payments. You may have personally paid some of these immediate bills to prevent repossession or other negative action by your loved one's creditors. If applicable, discuss this situation with the probate judge and request the court order reimbursement of these payments to you from the loved one's estate. Don't pay any debts that don't have to be paid immediately. Debts are required to be paid in the order of their priority and not until the claim period has ended. Failure to pay higher priority debts before lower priority debts may result in the executor becoming personally liable for the debt.

Validating the Will. During the initial hearing, the probate court judge may also determine whether the will is legally valid. For the will to be valid, your loved had to be of sound mind when he or she signed the will, knew and understood what property he or she had, and what it meant to leave it to someone. In addition, depending on the law of the state where your loved one resided, he or she must have signed and dated the will in front of a witness or witnesses. Most states require two witnesses to sign the will and acknowledge that your loved one signed the will. Usually, one of the witnesses can be the lawyer who drafted the will. Most states don't allow beneficiaries under the will to be witnesses. This type of will is referred to as a self-proving affidavit or self-proving will because it includes an affidavit or sworn statement signed by a witness or witnesses under the penalty of perjury attesting to the loved one's signature and the contents of the will.

A self-proving will may be admitted to probate without the testimony of the witness that signed the affidavit. In most cases, a self-proving affidavit or will provides enough evidence for the probate judge to validate the will and begin the probate process. In general, probate courts allow the following types of witness statements: (1) a self-proving affidavit as discussed previously, (2) a sworn statement signed by the witness at the time probate is opened, and (3) a personal statement made by the witness to the court. In addition, the court may accept other evidence of the will's validity, such as the testimony of someone who is familiar with your loved one's signature.

Note that all the beneficiaries listed in the will have a right to review the document and accept or object to it. The court decides how to move forward if the will is contested. If the will is contested, the executor needs to consider once again whether to seek assistance of a probate attorney.

Chapter Summary

Congratulations on learning when, where, and how to open probate and enduring the pressure involved in getting to this stage! The next stop on our journey involves determining your loved one's assets and debts as well as putting a value on them. This involves some snooping and detective work. As always, stay focused as we get closer to the finish line.

Chapter 8

Discover Your Loved One's Assets and Debts, Value the Estate

C ongratulations! You've performed many tasks that needed to be done and are well on your way toward settling your loved one's estate. Let's continue moving forward with the momentum you've built. In this chapter, you'll learn how to uncover and inventory your loved one's assets and debts as well as value your loved one's estate.

Keep Accurate Records

Before we start with the inventory and valuation process, it's a good time to remind you that it's essential to keep accurate records of all transactions related to your loved one's estate so you can correctly value the estate and comply with the executor's duties. Keeping accurate records is more than inventorying and recording your loved one's assets. It also involves recording all income received, all assets acquired or sold, and all expenses paid on behalf of the estate. As you perform an inventory of your loved one's estate, you may discover information about debts, liens, taxes, or other "obstacles" that may encumber or restrict ownership of your loved one's assets. Keep a record of this information on the sample Inventory List as well as the Debt and Expenses Paid Form included in the Appendix.

Pay Attention to Deadlines

As the executor, you have a certain amount of time after your loved one's passing (usually about 90 days, depending on your probate state) to inventory and record the assets. It's important to move forward quickly, but you must also move forward carefully. This means paying close attention to the documents you uncover during your inventory. These documents may contain deadlines for taking some kind of action after your loved one has passed away. For example, a life insurance policy may require you to notify the insurance company in writing of your loved one's passing within 30 days of death. As you perform the inventory and uncover information, take careful note of all deadlines, and calendar the date of each deadline. Take the time to satisfy the notification, or other required action, before the deadline. Notifying insurance companies, government agencies, and businesses or your loved one's death is discussed further in the next chapter.

Discover and Inventory Your Loved One's Assets

Once the probate court has appointed the executor, the executor must identify and inventory all the assets of the loved one's estate and provide a valuation of those assets. Your loved one's assets consist of the real and personal property he or she owned that have some value, including real estate, stocks, bonds, investment accounts, mortgages, notes and cash, personal and business bank accounts, life insurance, pensions, profit-sharing plans, annuities, retirement funds, motor vehicles, valuable jewelry, art, electronics, furniture, appliances, pets, and other items. Ideally, your loved one left you with a detailed list of his or her assets and where to find them. If this isn't the case, it will be up to you as the executor to uncover and inventory your loved one's real and personal property. If any of your loved one's property is in the hands of other people, the executor is required to collect this property and bring it back into the estate's control.

The Inventory List

The goal of inventorying your loved one's property is to become familiar with and account for every item that has value. You'll record these items in the sample Inventory List, included in the Appendix. Doing so will keep you organized, simplify the inventory process, and help you accomplish future tasks. Depending on the state where you filed probate, the probate court may require you to file a completed inventory list, which may be referred to as an "inventory form," with the probate court and provide the list to those who have an interest in the estate. Check with your probate court to see whether a specific inventory form is required and, if so, obtain a sample form from the court.

The completed Inventory List can also be used to perform the "final accounting," which is one of the last steps the executor performs. The final accounting is a summary of your loved one's assets and their associated values as well as a list of funds received and payments made on behalf of the estate. The final accounting period runs from the time your loved one passed away to the time you perform the final accounting. You'll learn how to perform the final accounting in Chapter 12.

Inventory Financial Assets

A large part of inventorying your loved one's estate will involve collecting and reviewing financial information to determine financial assets, which includes stocks, bonds, cryptocurrencies, investment accounts, mortgages, titles, promissory notes, cash, life insurance, pensions, profit-sharing plans, annuities, and retirement funds. If your loved one's financial assets aren't listed in the will, then uncovering these assets may be time-consuming and require some investigation. If necessary, set aside blocks of time each day to accomplish this task.

Most people have a system for maintaining and updating their financial files. Methods usually range from physical file folders to elaborate spreadsheets stored on a computer. Whatever method your loved one used, consider that as the starting point in piecing together his or her financial puzzle. Hard copies of financial paperwork may be found in folders in a desk, safe, or bank safe deposit box along with other important documents such as titles, deeds, and passports. There may be little in the way of hard copies, and most, or all, of your loved one's financial information may be stored on a computer's hard drive or the Cloud. It's also possible that your loved one opted out of receiving hard copies and chose to store statements and account information on the website of the service provider, such as the bank, investment provider, credit card issuer, and other account provider. Keep this in mind as you investigate your loved one's financial status. Be prepared to provide to the financial institution a certified copy of the death certificate and proof that you are a beneficiary of a specific financial account or the estate's executor or administrator, as shown in letters of administration or letters testamentary from the probate court (discussed in Chapter 7).

As you uncover your loved one's financial assets, list them and their associated value on the Inventory List. Of course, note whether any payment or other action is required and the deadline for such payment or action. Even if you think you've uncovered all your loved one's financial assets, proceed with the expectation that this financial history is incomplete. Treat the Inventory List as a fluid document and update it as necessary. You can revise it to add new assets you may uncover, adjust the value of an asset, record any lien related to the asset, and include other information.

Inventory Real Property

Your loved one's real property may be the estate's most valuable asset. Real property means real estate, including the land and any crops or structures on the land. Your loved one may have an owner-ship interest in the house that he or she lived in at the time of passing, a vacation house, investment property, timeshare, piece of land, or other real property. In addition, your loved one may be the sole owner of the property or may own the real property with others. The real property may be held in a trust or owned by a limited liability or other company. Further, the real property may be subject to a mortgage and a security interest held by a third party such as the mortgage lender.

Depending on the relationship you had with your loved one, you may feel you know the extent of the real property he or she owns. When my dad passed away, he was living in the house he had lived in for the past 50 years. My siblings and I had many conversations with him about his house; the status of his mortgage, which was paid off; and other issues. We knew his financial situation well and that this house was the only real property he owned. However, your situation may be different. If you have any doubts as to your loved one's ownership of real property, you need to perform a real property search to verify all real property your loved one may own.

Depending on your expertise, you may be able to perform this search yourself. However, a search of your loved one's real property is probably better left to a professional. The most accurate and thorough way to accomplish the search is by hiring a title company to perform it. The search's cost should be borne by your loved one's estate, and any out-of-pocket expense should be reimbursed by the estate at the appropriate time. As always, keep track of all expenses and save your receipts. Let's discuss performing the search yourself versus hiring a title company to do it for you.

Performing the Real Property Search Yourself. Uncovering ownership of your loved one's real property begins with reviewing the paperwork he or she has on hand. You're looking for all documents related to real property ownership. This includes loan and escrow statements, loan documents, purchase agreements, deeds of trust, titles, tax assessments, homeowner association documents, homeowner insurance policies, property tax receipts, and related bills and invoices. These documents are clues to the real property your loved one may own. Chances are you came across some of these documents when you were searching for the will.

Review these documents carefully with the goal of determining the real property your loved one may own. Also, look for important terms that require your immediate attention. These include mortgage, tax, or other payments related to the real property that may be coming due. Calendar all upcoming due dates, keep these documents in a file folder, and scan them to your computer's hard drive if possible.

After reviewing the documents your loved one has on hand, the next step is to perform a search of public records. Public records, such as tax and land records, contain information about real property ownership. The property tax assessment office in the county where the property exists will have updated ownership information for all properties that are assessed for property taxes in that county. The tax assessor updates ownership information as it changes. As a member of the general public, you're entitled to search information related to property assessment values and tax liens for free. Search for your loved one's name with the property tax assessor's office in each area where you think your loved one may own real property.

In addition to the tax assessor's office, the land records office contains listings of an area's real estate records. Property ownership documents, such as deeds of trust, are filed in the county's land records office. To search for real property ownership related to your loved one, contact the land records office in the county where you think your loved one may own real property. Methods for searching property records vary by area. You may be able to search the property records online at the office's official website by using your loved one's name. Otherwise, you may have to visit the office in person.

Hiring a Title Company to Search for Real Property. A quick and thorough way to uncover the real property your loved one owns involves using a title company. For a fee, a title company will perform statewide searches to identify properties your loved one owns. If you think your loved one may own real property you aren't aware of, then hiring a title company to perform a comprehensive search is the way to go. You can find names and recommendations for title companies by contacting a local realtor. Realtors work closely with title companies and are more than happy to provide you with recommendations. Try to get more than one recommendation. Call the title companies recommended by the realtors and compare their services and fees.

Determining Real Property Payments. Your loved one's ownership interest in his or her real property may be subject to a mortgage, promissory note, or other loan. If so, there's probably a security interest and lien held by the lender related to the property. Typically, this allows the lender to foreclose on the property if payments aren't made or other conditions of the loan aren't met. It's important for you to determine whether your loved one's real property is subject to a mortgage and to learn the details about any upcoming payments or other obligations. In most cases, you want to make sure that loan payments are timely made to the lender to protect the ownership interest of your loved one's estate.

Likewise, you need to determine the details of any real property taxes, insurance, and other payments related to the real property that may be coming due. If there's a mortgage on the real property, there's a good likelihood that the real property taxes and property insurance payments are set up in an escrow account. This means that part of the monthly loan payment is allocated to cover real property taxes, insurance premiums, and other costs. Under this circumstance, you don't pay these expenses separately because they're included as part of the mortgage payment. The lender's escrow department will have this information on file. After you determine the details of these payments, make sure to add the payment and other information to your Inventory List. Notifying mortgage companies of your loved one's death is discussed further in Chapter 9.

Inventory Personal Possessions

A large part of determining your loved one's assets involves inventorying his or her personal possessions. Accomplish this inventory simply by going through his or her home, storage unit, or similar place. Depending on your loved one, this should be a relatively straightforward process, although it may be time consuming.

As you go through your loved one's possessions, list them on the Inventory List. You don't have to list smaller, knick-knack items individually, although it may be helpful to group them together on the Inventory List. Because you're familiar with the contents of the will, this is a good time to identify items that your loved intended for a particular person, referred to as specific bequests. Make sure to set them aside. Depending on the quantity of your loved one's personal property, you may want to physically group things by category. Items such as jewelry, kitchen items, artwork, and furniture can be easily grouped together. You may list larger items on the Inventory List and note their location. Note whether any payment or other required action is related to the personal possession.

Going through your loved one's personal items may unleash a lifetime of emotions related to these items. The contents of my mom and dad's home brought to life memories spanning many years. It was emotional but also uplifting, as I remembered the great times we had together. Consider this task of inventorying your loved one's personal property a part of the healing process. Although you may not feel comfortable going through these possessions, realize it's a necessary part of your duties as the executor. Your loved one knew this would happen someday, and you were chosen as the perfect person to accomplish this task.

Consider Your Loved One's Personal Loans to Others

Your loved one may have loaned money to a friend, family member, or heir. These loans are debts owed to the estate and are considered assets of the estate. If you know of such a loan, you need to attempt to collect the debt. As the executor, you don't have the authority to cancel the debt. If the loan was to an heir of your loved one, then the heir can either repay the estate the amount owed, or you can deduct it from the inheritance the heir would have been entitled to had there been no loan. An exception would be if there's evidence the debt was canceled by your loved one, possibly in writing or in the will. For example, if an heir was to receive a $10,000 distribution from the estate but owes the estate $5,000, and the debt wasn't canceled by your loved one, then that heir is entitled to a net distribution of $5,000, and the debt to the estate is considered satisfied.

Jointly Owned Property

Jointly owned property is property owned by two or more parties, typically spouses. The form of the title to the joint property, as evidenced by the property's title or deed, will determine how it will be transferred upon a loved one's death. Many states have special types of joint ownership with rights of survivorship. For instance, if the property is held as a "joint tenancy with a right of survivorship" or as a "tenancy in the entirety," then the property may automatically transfer to the surviving joint owner upon the loved one's death. Depending on the state, these types of joint ownership may only apply to real property. Community property, which is discussed later in this chapter, is another type of joint ownership exclusive to spouses in community property states. Community property typically has a right of survivorship and transfers automatically to the surviving joint owner or beneficiary.

In many cases, if the jointly owned property isn't owned with a right of survivorship, then the owners are considered tenants in common. Tenants in common own a specific percentage of the jointly owned property. For example, two owners may hold the jointly owned property as a "tenancy in common" with each owning 50 percent of the property. If one of the tenants in common dies, his or her 50 percent ownership passes to the decedent's heirs per the terms of the will, or according to the intestacy laws of the loved one's state if he or she died without a will.

Retirement Plans

Surviving spouses may also have vested or assigned rights in their loved one's retirement plan, individual retirement account (IRA), and 401(k) plan. For a 401(k) plan, the surviving spouse is the presumed beneficiary of the loved one's 401(k) account at death. Under federal law, the surviving spouse receives the total amount of the 401(k) account unless the surviving spouse waived the right to receive the proceeds of the 401(k) plan in writing. Likewise, a spouse can't remove the other spouse as a beneficiary from the plan without the other spouse's written consent. IRA accounts are treated differently and don't require a spouse to name the other spouse as the account's beneficiary. However, state law may give the surviving spouse the right to receive an amount equal to the amount of the loved one's total assets as an elective share.

Rights of a Surviving Spouse—Family Entitlements

Many states provide surviving spouses and some family members with certain entitlements upon death. These rights vary from state to state, depending on the state's law where your loved one resided at the time of death. Family entitlements may have priority over creditor's claims other than funeral expenses and expenses associated with the administration of your loved one's estate. In community property states, the surviving spouse may already own the community property from the marriage. Some of the rights of a surviving spouse may include an elective share, family allowance, personal property allowances, exempt property, rights to the family residence, and other rights. If you're the surviving spouse of your loved one, make sure to check what specific rights you may have under your state's law.

Elective Share

An elective share is a share of a loved one's estate that a surviving spouse may claim in place of what the spouse was left in the will. A surviving spouse may choose to take an elective share when he or she (1) is left out of the will or (2) the elective share is larger than the surviving spouse will receive under the will. The law of the state where the loved one resided upon death will determine what the surviving spouse is entitled to and the amount of the elective share. Depending on the state, the elective share may be based on the length of the surviving spouse and loved one's marriage, the existence of any minor children or dependent adults, and the surviving spouse's wealth. If you're a surviving spouse of the loved one, be sure to investigate the elective share in the state where the loved one resided at death and whether the election may be right for you depending on your personal situation.

Family Allowance

A surviving spouse, minor children, and dependent adults may also be entitled to a family allowance from the loved one's estate to help support them during the administration of the estate. The amount of the family allowance is paid by the loved one's estate and varies from state to state. If you're a surviving spouse of the loved one, check what the family allowance may be in the state where your loved one resided at death.

Exempt Property

Exempt property is property that a loved one's creditors aren't entitled to if the loved one had a surviving spouse or other descendants. Examples of exempt property may include motor vehicles, personal possessions below a certain value, household furnishings, kitchen appliances, clothes, college savings plans, and other items. Again, if you're a surviving spouse of the loved one, find out what property may be exempt in the state where your loved one resided at death.

Value Your Loved One's Assets

Once you've inventoried your loved one's personal property (financial assets and personal possessions) and real property, you need to assign a fair market value to that property. Fair market value is the price a person reasonably interested in purchasing an item would be willing to pay for it.

Valuing a financial asset is usually straightforward if you have a recent statement or other account information telling you the current amount of each account. If you can't determine the value of the financial asset after reviewing account and other information, as well as communicating with the financial institution, you may have to make a good faith, reasoned estimate of its value. A financial asset's value may fluctuate as interest rates and returns on investments change, payments are made, and other events occur. Nevertheless, list the financial asset and its associated value in the Inventory List as accurately as possible.

The internet is a useful source for valuing personal possessions. You can determine the fair market value of a motor vehicle by pricing it on a website such as the National Automobile Dealers Association (www.nada.com), Kelley Blue Book (www.kbb.com), or Edmunds (www.edmunds.com). These companies are well respected, and the values they place on vehicles are generally accepted as their fair market value.

It may be more difficult to place an accurate fair market value on your loved one's electronics, jewelry, art, and other personal property. Investigating the price which other people are selling similar items for is a useful way to determine the value of your loved one's property. Websites such as eBay (www.ebay.com) and Craigslist (www.craigslist.com) show the prices for which people are listing their personal property. Of course, the listing price may vary greatly from the price a buyer will actually pay for an item, and you never really know an item's worth until someone buys the item. Your goal is simply to attempt to place a reasonable value on your loved one's personal property based on what a person is likely to pay for the property. Keep in mind that much of the personal property may have intrinsic value; it may be valuable to you but have little or no resale value. Just value the object as accurately as you can without considering its intrinsic value.

In most cases, you'll be able to place a fair market value on an asset without hiring a professional appraiser. However, if you uncover an item that you believe to be valuable but can't place a value on the item, a certified appraiser can perform the valuation. Examples include vintage cars, elaborate jewelry, and artwork. Similarly, valuing a business is usually a complicated task beyond the average person's ability, so an appraiser's training and knowledge may be necessary. With regard to real property, ask a local realtor to assist you with valuing your loved one's home or any other real property he or she owns.

After you determine your loved one's assets and place a value on them, the assets will later be used to pay your loved one's legitimate debts at the appropriate time, as discussed in Chapter 10. After paying legitimate debts, the executor will distribute your loved one's remaining assets to the beneficiaries, as discussed in Chapter 11.

Determine Digital Assets and Contact the Providers

Digital assets encompass a variety of information stored online, in the Cloud, or on a computer's hard drive. Examples of digital assets include the following:

- Email accounts with Yahoo, Gmail, Hotmail, and other providers;
- Social media accounts such as Facebook, Twitter, Instagram, TikTok, and LinkedIn;
- Online merchant accounts like Amazon, eBay, and PayPal; and
- Bank statements, credit card accounts, financial records, tax records, medical records, and photographs.

Generally, an electronic service provider like those listed previously aren't permitted to intentionally divulge the contents of any digital account to anyone other than the account holder or his or her agent. As an executor administering your loved one's estate, you need the proper authority to access certain digital assets. Otherwise, you may be in violation of state and federal law. Many states recognize the dilemma an executor faces regarding digital assets and have enacted legislation giving executors legal authority to manage their loved one's digital assets and electronic communications. To avoid any violations, you need to review the user agreements that your loved has with his or her various electronic service providers. Then notify each provider of your loved one's death, your position as executor, and your intent to access your loved one's account and digital information to close the account and settle the estate. Ask providers for their assistance in accessing your loved one's digital account. They deal with these situations every day.

Some providers allow the executor to access the loved one's account if the loved one consented to the executor's access in his or her will, a power of attorney, or when he or she signed up for the account. For example, Facebook allows its users to name a "legacy contact" who is given access to the user's profile when Facebook is notified of the user's death. PayPal allows an executor to close the deceased's account once a request is made in writing and accompanied by a photo identification of the executor, a copy of the executor's legal authorization, and a copy of the death certificate. Otherwise, you may need an order from the probate court allowing you to access, and close, the account.

Obtain an Employer Identification Number for Your Loved One's Estate

All estates are required to obtain an Employer Identification Number (EIN), also known as a "tax ID number." The EIN is similar to a social security number and identifies your loved one's estate to the Internal Revenue Service (IRS). The estate and your loved one are two distinct taxable entities. You will need the EIN to file the required IRS Form 1041 for your loved one's estate. The easiest and quickest way for most people to obtain an estate EIN is by completing the Estate EIN form on the IRS's website. It's a simple, one-page form. The IRS will provide you with the EIN number for your loved one's estate the same day you submit the Estate EIN form. Otherwise, you need to complete a copy of IRS Form SS-4, mail it to the IRS, and wait for the EIN to arrive in the mail.

Open a Bank Account for Your Loved One's Estate

Your loved one's estate is responsible for paying the debts of your loved one, including any income tax and estate taxes that are owed. Utility, rent, mortgage, and other payments also must be paid as they come due. When your loved one passed away, you may not have had authority to write checks from his or her account. The exception would be if you were a joint account holder or had a financial power of attorney that permitted you to control your loved one's bank account at the time of his or her death and that power didn't "dissolve" upon the death. Assuming these exceptions don't apply, you should open a bank account in the name of the estate, with you named as executor, to pay bills and accept deposits. To do this, you will need a copy of the death certificate, the estate's EIN, and evidence of your authority to act as executor as shown by the Letters of Administration or Letters Testamentary you received from the probate court. Until the estate's bank account is opened, you may have to personally pay some of the estate's bills, such as the mortgage and utility bills, as they come due. Keep track of the expenses you pay on behalf of your loved one's estate and request reimbursement of these expenditures by the estate from the probate court.

File Form 56 with the IRS

You should file Form 56 with the IRS on two occasions. Your first filing of Form 56 notifies the IRS that you are executor of your loved one's estate and that all tax correspondence related to your loved one and the estate should be sent to you. This should be done shortly after you have been named executor of your loved one's estate. The second time you file Form 56 with the IRS will be after you've settled the estate, completed your duties as executor, and are terminating your responsibilities. This second filing may give you certain long-term legal protections.

Note that IRS Form 1310 is used to claim a federal tax refund for the surviving spouse or another beneficiary of a loved one. This form notifies the IRS that a taxpayer has died and directs it to send the refund to the beneficiary.

Protect Your Loved One's Assets

One of your jobs as the executor is to protect your loved one's property from loss. That means you must take reasonable steps to keep the property safe. Let your common sense guide you. Make sure the area where the property is being kept is safe, locked, protected from the elements, and heated and cooled as necessary depending on the property you're protecting. Also, don't allow relatives or other people to remove items until your loved one's property has been distributed per the terms of the will, creditors have been paid, and the probate process is complete.

Protect Your Loved One's Identity

You may think identity theft only happens to people while they are alive, but identity theft also occurs in death. The obituary gives identity thieves notice of your loved one's death. As discussed in the following section, you can help prevent identity theft by promptly notifying credit reporting agencies, the Social Security Administration, banks, insurance companies, credit card companies, and other businesses of your loved one's death. The business or agency will probably require a copy of your loved one's death certificate as evidence of his or her passing. Call their offices or visit their websites to verify what they require for proof of your loved one's death. It may be a letter from the executor, a copy of the death certificate, or both. The Appendix includes several sample notification-of-death letters you can revise for your circumstances. Send your letters to the appropriate agencies and businesses by certified U.S. mail, return receipt requested, and keep a copy of each letter for your file. Now it's time to determine your loved one's debts and creditors.

Determine Your Loved One's Debts and Creditors

As the executor, you're responsible for settling your loved one's debts, which are also called "liabilities." The first step is to gather all the information you can about your loved one's debts and related creditors. You likely came across documents, emails, or other information indicating possible debts and creditors when you were inventorying your loved one's property. Typical creditors include mortgage lenders, credit card companies, utility companies, automobile finance companies, banks, and other lenders. Credit reporting agencies also are a good source for uncovering your loved one's debts.

Use the information you uncover to prepare a list of your loved one's debts, creditor names, the type of debt owed to the creditor (credit card, mortgage, utility, etc.), the due date and amount of any payment, and the balance or total amount of the debt. Use the Debt and Expenses Paid Form in the Appendix to help you list and organize your loved one's debts and creditors.

Bills That Need to Be Paid Immediately

Earlier in this chapter you learned how to obtain an EIN for your loved one's estate and open a bank account in the name of the estate with you listed as the executor. In Chapters 9 and 10 you'll learn about contacting your loved one's creditors and paying debts in order of priority after the claim period has ended. However, your loved one may have bills that are currently due or will be due shortly—maybe even before you obtained an EIN, opened the bank account, or contacted creditors.

Your loved one's immediate bills may include mortgage, rent, utility, insurance, car, tax, and other payments. Your goal is to avoid any activity by a creditor that may result in a loss to the estate by way of repossession, lien, or other negative action. To avoid this situation, you may have to make some immediate payments to creditors. Keep track of these payments and request the court order reimbursement of these payments to you from the loved one's estate.

Don't pay any debts that don't have to be paid immediately. Debts are required to be paid in the order of their priority and not until the claim period has ended. Failure to pay higher priority debts before lower priority debts may result in the executor becoming personally liable for the debt. You'll learn about this in Chapter 10.

Joint Debts

Generally, your loved one's debts aren't the debts of his or her family or other people (although they are debts of your loved one's estate). However, if your loved one had a joint account with another person then the creditor may look to the other person to satisfy the joint debt. A joint account is one in which two people individually agree to the terms of a loan or other agreement and can be held individually liable for the account's debts. A joint account is a situation where two people (e.g., the "buyer" and the "co-buyer" or "co-signer") enter into an agreement for joint credit or for the joint purchase of an item, such as a car. The buyer would be considered the primary debtor on the contract, and the co-buyer or co-signer would be the secondary debtor. If the buyer fails to make a payment on the property, the lender may demand payment from the co-buyer or co-signer per the terms of the agreement. An additional card holder, as opposed to a co-buyer or co-signer, isn't responsible for the loved one's debt because they didn't guarantee the debt's payment.

To confirm the rights of the creditor, buyer, and co-buyer or co-signer, read the credit agreement on the joint account. The state in which your loved one's estate is being probated may also have laws limiting the creditor's right to collect a debt on a deceased's joint account. Even if the account is a joint account, be sure to notify the creditor of your loved one's passing. Discuss any outstanding issues with the creditor, including whether you want to continue using the account and whether they will forgive the amount owed on the debt.

Community Property

Issues regarding liability or responsibility for your loved one's debts also arise if your loved one was married and resided in a "community property" state. Community property is property owned in common by husband and wife; they have an undivided one-half interest in the property based on their marital status. Current community property states include Arizona, California, Idaho, Louisiana, Nevada, New Mexico, Texas, and Washington. Most other states are classified as "common law" jurisdictions.

The difference between community property and common law systems is based on the property rights possessed by married people. In a common law state system, each spouse owns whatever he or she earns. Under a community property system, one half of the earnings of each spouse is considered owned by the other spouse. Similarly, in a community property state, one spouse may be liable for the debts of another even if they didn't agree to them. If your loved one was married and resided in a community property state, then his or her spouse may be responsible for a portion of your loved one's debts. In this situation, I encourage you to contact an attorney knowledgeable about the community property laws in your loved one's state.

Chapter Summary

This chapter taught you how to uncover your loved one's assets, value the assets, protect the assets, shield your loved one's identity, and determine debts and creditors. You wore several hats, did some heavy lifting, and accomplished some amazing tasks. You're making great progress and need to keep your momentum going! Your hard work and persistence will be rewarded soon. In the next chapter, I'll show you how to use the information you just uncovered about your loved one's assets and debts to notify creditors and different agencies of your loved one's passing. These tasks are straightforward and may be performed quickly with little stress. Let's get started!

Chapter 9

Notify Creditors, Social Security, Insurance Companies, the Public, and Others

In Chapter 4, we talked about informing family members, friends, and others with close family ties about your loved one's passing. You made a list of people to contact in order of importance. However, you may have chosen not to speak with creditors and other organizations at that time. Even though your loved one has passed away, his or her creditors have the right to seek payment of your loved one's debts from the estate. The creditors may not know your loved one passed away and you, as executor, may not know who all of your loved one's creditors are. Nonetheless, you're required to timely notify all known and unknown creditors of your loved one's death, that probate has been opened, and that they have a certain amount of time to come forward with any claims.

General Communication Tips

Initial communications to the businesses and agencies should be made by telephone. That way, you can quickly inform the organization of your loved one's death and discuss the next steps in obtaining your loved one's account information, agreements between the organization and your loved one, the organization's notice of death and other requirements, applicable deadlines, possibly closing the account, and other issues. It's important to take detailed notes of your telephone calls with these organizations, including who you spoke with and their contact information, what was discussed, when the conversation occurred, required follow-up, and anything else that may be meaningful. If important information was discussed in the telephone conversation, send a letter or email to the person you spoke with restating what was discussed. Important information includes the discussion of benefits, agreements, actions that the other person is supposed to take, deadlines and extensions, and any other issues you may need to rely on in the future.

Following up a verbal discussion with an email or letter is referred to as "memorializing" your conversation. The follow-up letter or email provides a written history of what was discussed and can be referenced if there is a dispute regarding the conversation. If the person you spoke with sends you written correspondence memorializing the conversation, read it carefully to ensure its accuracy. If it isn't accurate, send an email or letter to the person stating how his or her letter was inaccurate. Be sure to send your letters and any attachments, such as death certificates, by certified U.S. mail, return receipt requested. Keep a copy of the letter, attachments, and proof of mailing in your files. Note that these follow-up letters memorializing conversations are in addition to, not in place of, the notice of death letters you must send and publish to creditors.

Determine Notification Requirements

Depending on the probate court in the county where you filed probate, notice requirements will vary as to how notice must be given to known creditors and the contents that must be included in the notice. To determine unknown creditors, you likely will be required to publish a notice of death and deadline to file claims for a certain amount of time in the local newspaper where your loved one resided. You may need to file proof of the notices you mailed and published with the probate court, including an affidavit from the newspaper of the publication dates. It's your responsibility as executor to determine the notice requirements of the probate court where you opened probate and to strictly comply with these requirements. In addition, individual creditors, insurance companies, and other entities may have their own notice requirements you need to comply with. Ask the individual organizations about their requirements when you call them.

Notify Creditors and Others of Your Loved One's Passing and Deadline to File Claims

The Debt and Expenses Paid Form you completed in Chapter 8 should contain the names of your loved one's known creditors discovered through your investigation of his or her debts. Review the form one more time to make sure it contains all known debts and creditors. Armed with this information and the creditor and probate court's notice requirements, you'll now notify employers, business partners, credit reporting agencies, the Social Security Administration, known and unknown creditors, insurance companies, utility companies, and others of your loved one's passing. Plan to notify all these persons and entities in writing of your loved one's passing within 30 days of death, as there may be deadlines for submitting claims for death benefits.

The Appendix includes sample notice letters to help make this task relatively straightforward and stress-free. Revise the letters to fit your situation and the notice requirements of your loved one's creditors, insurance companies and other entities, and the requirements of the applicable probate court. Creditors, the Social Security Administration, and other entities will require you to provide proof of your loved one's death and your legal authority to receive the information. The signed Letters of Administration or Letters Testamentary that you received from the probate court, together with a copy of the death certificate, provide such proof and legal authority.

Deadlines for Creditors to File Claims Against Your Loved One's Estate

Generally, creditors must come forward by the claim deadline to present their alleged claims against the estate. If they fail to do so they forfeit their right to collect the alleged debt. State law imposes strict deadlines for creditors to file claims to ensure the estate is administered and closed in a timely fashion. The amount of time a creditor has to present its claim is governed by the state in which you opened probate. A typical claim period is three to six months. As usual, contact the probate court where you opened probate for information to help you determine exactly how much time a creditor is given to present a claim against your loved one's estate. Include this claim period in your notice to creditors as previously discussed and calendar the deadline as your reminder.

Notify Your Loved One's Employer or Business Partner

Considering the relative "closeness" that many employers have with their employees, there's a good likelihood your loved one's employer, if any, already knows of his or her passing. This is even more true if your loved one had a business partner. However, your investigation of assets and debts may have uncovered some previously unknown form of partnership your loved one had with another party. Even if you previously informed your loved one's employer or business partner of the passing, you likely will need to speak with them again to gather more information. For example, there may be employee wages (paychecks), a pension or savings plan, company life insurance policy, an ownership position, or other asset or debt your loved one's estate is legally entitled to and for which you must account.

Depending on your loved one's relationship and ownership position with the employer or partner, you should speak with them in person or at least by telephone. Discuss any contracts, obligations, wage statements, benefits, pensions, saving plans, and ownership your loved one may have with the business. The employer or partner may ask you for information and documentation verifying your loved one's death and your authority to act on his or her behalf. The signed Letters of Administration or Letters Testamentary that you received from the probate court, together with a copy of the death certificate, provide such proof and legal authority. Don't forget to exchange contact information in case an unforeseen issue arises in the future.

As always, take detailed notes of your communications so you don't have to rely solely on your memory. Thoroughly review all documents provided by the employer or business partner and contact an attorney if you have any questions. Revise your Inventory List and Debt and Expenses Paid Form as needed to add newly discovered assets or debts.

Notify the "Big Three" Credit Reporting Agencies

The big three credit reporting agencies are Experian, Equifax, and TransUnion. They need to be notified of your loved one's death as soon as possible. Request that the credit reporting agency flag your loved one's account with the following statement: "Deceased: Do not issue credit." This will help prevent identity theft. The Appendix includes a sample notice of death to a credit reporting agency. You'll include a copy of the death certificate and signed Letters of Administration or Letters Testamentary with your notification to the credit reporting agency. Send your letters and attachments to the credit reporting agencies by certified U.S. mail, return receipt requested.

When you contact the credit reporting agencies, also request a copy of your loved one's credit report. Reviewing these credit reports is often the most accurate way to find out exactly what debts were outstanding at the time of your loved one's passing. If the credit report shows an open balance with any previously unknown lender, contact that lender and request information and proof of the debt. Update the Inventory List and Debt and Expenses Paid Form with any new information you uncover from the credit reports. The current mailing addresses and telephone numbers for the big three credit reporting agencies are as follows:

-TransUnion
P.O. Box 2000
Chester, PA 19022
800-916-8800
-Experian
P.O. Box 2002

Allen, TX 75013

888-397-3742

-Equifax

P.O. Box 740260

Atlanta, GA 30374

800-465-7166

These addresses and telephone numbers are subject to change, so double-check the address before you send your certified letter.

Notify Social Security and Determine Possible Social Security Benefits

Contact the Social Security Administration to let it know your loved one has died and that any future Social Security benefits to your loved one should stop (otherwise you will have to pay them back). You also need to find out if there are any Social Security benefits available to surviving family members.

Certain family members may qualify for a one-time death benefit or monthly benefits. This depends, in part, on your loved one's work history and the length of time he or she was employed in jobs insured under Social Security. Currently, Social Security pays a one-time benefit to the surviving spouse if they were living with the loved one. If there's no surviving spouse, a child of the loved one may be eligible for the one-time benefit. In addition, certain family members may be eligible to receive monthly benefits. These family members include the following:

- A surviving spouse age 60 or older (age 50 or older if disabled);
- A surviving spouse of any age that is caring for the loved one's child who is under age 16 or disabled;
- An unmarried child of the loved one who is younger than age 18 (or up to age 19 if they are a full-time student in an elementary or secondary school) or age 18 or older with a disability that began before age 22;

- A stepchild, grandchild, step-grandchild, or adopted child under certain circumstances;
- Parents, age 62 or older, who were dependent on the loved one for at least half of their support; and
- A surviving divorced spouse under certain circumstances.

If you used a funeral home to help with your loved one's death, the funeral director may have already reported the death to the Social Security Administration. Check with the funeral director to see if this was done. Even if it was done, you will want to contact Social Security to determine the availability of any benefits for your loved one's family. Be persistent with your communications to Social Security, as its rules are complicated, and not all of its representatives are well-versed. It may take time to determine possible benefits. Contact Social Security by telephone at 800-772-1213 and take notes of your conversation. Be sure to send all letters and attachments to the Social Security Administration by certified U.S. mail, return receipt requested. The Appendix includes a sample notice of death letter to the Social Security Administration. Related information and frequently asked questions are available online at www.ssa.gov/plan ners/survivors.

Notify Insurance Companies

Your earlier investigation of your loved one's assets, debts, and other information likely revealed information regarding motor vehicle, homeowners, accident/health, business, or life insurance coverage related to your loved one. Depending on your loved one's situation, he or she may not have all these different insurance coverages. If your loved one didn't drive or own a business or real property, there likely won't be a motor vehicle, business, or homeowners' insurance policy. Also, because of the expense of insurance premiums, possible health problems, and other circumstances, it isn't unusual for older people to forego life insurance coverage unless they have a unique circumstance such as minor or disabled children. No matter the situation, a thorough investigation of potential insurance policies related to your loved one needs to be performed. This includes reviewing the insurance policies, determining possible insurance benefits (including funeral expenses), and notifying the insurance companies of your loved one's passing.

Your first contact with the insurance company should be by telephone. Typically, insurance companies require notification within 30 days of the passing. Be prepared to provide a certified copy of the death certificate and Letters of Administration or Letters Testamentary by certified U.S. Mail, return receipt requested.

If you have uncovered the name of your loved one's insurance agent, telephone the agent and advise him or her of your loved one's passing. Ask the agent about your loved one's insurance coverage; benefits, including death and funeral benefits; how to make a claim for benefits, including necessary paperwork; deadlines for submitting claims; whether any of the policies (e.g., homeowners and auto) may be put in the name of the surviving spouse or another person; how to cancel the insurance policies after any benefits are paid; and anything else you don't understand.

If there is any insurance coverage you weren't aware of, ask the agent for a copy of the related policy. Review each insurance policy and note its coverage and benefits. Certain insurance policies, such as homeowners and automobile policies, may have "carry-over" provisions for surviving spouses that allow them to maintain the policy by continuing to make premium payments.

The Appendix includes a sample notice of death letter to insurance companies. Revise and use it to fit your circumstances. Be sure to send your letters and attachments to the insurance companies by certified U.S. mail, return receipt requested. Also, update the Inventory List and Debt and Expenses Paid Form to include new information, such as death benefits or other insurance proceeds, provided by the insurance policies. If there is a dispute with the insurance company about benefits, especially if the company denies benefits you think your loved one's estate is entitled, promptly contact a lawyer for advice.

Notify Banks, Credit Card Companies, and Other Known Creditors

Earlier investigation of your loved one's assets and debts likely uncovered your loved one's potential bank accounts, bank loans, credit card accounts, automobile loans, various other debts, and creditors. Contact these businesses and creditors and notify them of your loved one's passing. Your first contact should be by telephone, with a follow-up letter by U.S. Mail return receipt requested as needed. The Appendix includes a sample notice of death to credit card companies letter, which you should revise to fit your circumstances. In addition to notifying the business of your loved one's passing, request the status of each account, the account balance, whether there are any upcoming payments due to the business, the process for disbursing any funds, and how to close the account. Under most circumstances, you should close each account unless it's held jointly by another person or some other reason exists for keeping the account open.

Notify Mortgage Companies

The relatively high cost of a house or other real property prevents most people from paying cash for a property. Instead, the buyer usually enters into an agreement with a lender to finance the property's purchase. This loan is often in the form of a mortgage, which is an interest in real property created by a written contract. Most mortgage terms require the borrower to repay the loan in installment payments over a certain period and at a certain interest rate. The mortgage lender maintains a security interest in the real property, and the property serves as collateral for the loan. If the borrower fails to comply with the terms of the loan, the lender is entitled to foreclose on (take possession) and sell the property.

If review of your loved one's assets indicates he or she owns a home or has an ownership interest in other real property, such as a vacation property or timeshare, then you need to determine if there is a mortgage or other loan related to the property. If your loved one was older at the time of passing, he or she may own the real property outright rather than having a mortgage related to the property. However, if your loved one has a mortgage and passed away before paying off the mortgage, the mortgage lender still has the right to all money due under the mortgage.

Similar to notifying your loved one's other creditors, promptly notify all mortgage lenders of your loved one's passing. Request the status of the account, including the amount of any upcoming payments and their due dates as well as the lender's standard operating procedure when a borrower dies. Ask the lender for copies of the mortgage documents so you can review them. You need to understand the important terms of the documents, such as the outstanding balance, payoff date, interest rate, all borrowers on the loan, and what happens when a borrower passes away. The mortgage may state that it can't be assigned to anyone unless that person can qualify for the mortgage. These are issues that need to be discussed with the mortgage lender, depending on your plans for the property.

As always, initially speak with the lender via telephone and keep detailed notes of any conversations. Send any correspondence to the mortgage lender by certified U.S. mail, return receipt requested. The mortgage lender likely will require a certified copy of your loved one's death certificate and Letters of Administration or Letters Testamentary as proof of your authority to act as executor.

Often there is more than one borrower on a mortgage loan. A typical scenario involves a couple buying a house with one person being the buyer or borrower and the other person being the co-buyer or co-borrower. Both people are responsible for complying with the terms of the mortgage loan. Depending on the terms of the loan and the state your loved resided at the time of passing, your loved one's interest in the house may pass automatically to the other surviving person, and the surviving person takes over the terms of the mortgage agreement. In a community property state like California, the property officially becomes the sole property of the surviving spouse. If the surviving person can't afford to make the mortgage payments, he or should discuss arrangements for loan payments with the lender. In the end, the surviving person may need to sell the house to pay off the mortgage and avoid foreclosure.

Similarly, a beneficiary who inherits a loved one's house, or other real property, may be forced to sell the property because the mortgage payments aren't affordable or the terms of the mortgage prevent assigning the mortgage to a third party. That means the mortgage may not transfer to the beneficiary unless the beneficiary can qualify for the mortgage.

When selling the property, be sure to consider whether there will be a difference between the proceeds from the sale of the property and the amount owed the lender under the mortgage loan. If the sale's proceeds are less than the amount due under the mortgage, then the estate or the property's beneficiary may be liable to the mortgage lender for the difference between the amount due under the mortgage and the sale's proceeds. On the other hand, if the proceeds from the sale of the property exceed the amount due under the mortgage, the estate or the property's beneficiary is entitled to that amount.

After you have reviewed and understand the terms of the mortgage or other loan, take the necessary time to consider whether you want to keep or sell the real property. A local real estate agent can help you determine the value of the property, whether any repairs are recommended prior to listing it for sale, the average number of days similar properties are taking to sell in the area, and other useful information.

When my father died, the house in which we were raised and my father had lived in for over 40 years had substantially deteriorated. We knew it was in a desirable area, and the market was advantageous to sellers. We spoke with several local real estate agents about the house, selling options, and the real estate market in general. After considering the information and performing our own research, we ended up hiring a contractor to remodel the home. This required money to hire the contractor and a waiting period to list the house for sale. Not everyone can afford this option. However, we sold the house for thousands of dollars more than we would have been able to sell it for without the renovations. The point is to research your options, discuss them with the heirs, and determine what makes the best sense for all involved to get the best return on your loved one's investment.

Notify Unknown Creditors—Public Notice

Depending on the state where your loved one lived when he or she passed away, certain facts regarding the death must be made public. Providing notice of your loved one's death to potential creditors allows them the opportunity to make a claim against the estate. The information contained in the notice will include basic information about your loved one's estate, the executor's name, mailing address and telephone number, the county where probate has been opened and the corresponding probate court's case number, where to submit claims against the estate, the deadline for submitting claims, and other information. Typically, the notice of death must be published for three consecutive weeks in the county newspaper that serves the area where your loved one lived. Unknown creditors that previously haven't been directly notified of your loved one's death have a certain amount of time, such as six months, to file claims against the estate.

Notice requirements vary as to how, where, and for how long the notice must be published and what facts must be contained in the public notice. Depending on the probate court in your county, you may need to file proof of the notices you mailed and published, including an affidavit from the newspaper of the publication dates. It's your responsibility as executor to determine what is required by the probate court where you opened probate. As always, start with your local probate for self-help forms and instructions as to publication requirements. Verify these requirements before publishing the notice of death. As with all other documentation, retain copies of all receipts, affidavits, and notices to creditors.

Notify Landlords

If your loved one rented a house, condominium, apartment, or other property at the time of his or her passing, promptly notify the landlord of your loved one's passing and request the lease or rental agreement. Depending on the landlord, lease agreement, and state where the rental property is located, your loved one's estate may be held liable for the remaining unpaid payments due under the lease. However, a compassionate landlord will work with the executor to end the lease early, although any security deposit may be used to pay unpaid rent, damage to the unit beyond reasonable wear and tear, and cleaning costs. As always, your initial conversation should be by telephone with a follow-up letter to the landlord that includes the death certificate and Letters of Administration or Letters Testamentary.

Notify Utility Providers and the Post Office

If your loved one owned or leased a house or other real property and was responsible for paying utility costs, you'll need to notify each utility of his or her passing and arrange to have the account closed or transferred. Typical utilities include water, sewer, electric, gas, cable/satellite television, trash, telephone, and the post office.

Unless you're living at your loved one's address, you should stop mail from being sent to his or her address. Contact the local post office where your loved one received mail and request the mail be forwarded to your address. This will accomplish several things. First, it will ensure you're aware of important documents and notices. Second, reviewing your loved one's mail will help you confirm you are aware of all your loved one's creditors, potential assets, and accounts that need to be paid or canceled. Third, it will keep mail from piling up at your loved one's home and reduce the appearance of a vacant home. In addition, you can register your loved one's name with the Data & Marketing Association, which maintains a Deceased Do Not Contact List. It may take several months for the advertising mail to stop being delivered. The post office and other utilities will require a copy of the death certificate and Letters of Administration or Letters Testamentary.

Cancel Your Loved One's Passport

If you'd like, you can keep your loved one's passport as a reminder of his or her traveling adventures or the good times you had together. However, considering the possibility of identity theft, the best practice is to mail the passport to the U.S. Department of State along with a copy of the death certificate and Letters of Administration or Letters Testamentary. Request that your loved one's passport be officially canceled. If you want the canceled passport returned, include a letter requesting its return and include an envelope with your address and enough postage to cover mailing. You can also ask the government to destroy the passport after it's canceled.

Cancel Your Loved One's Driver's License

To reduce the possibility of identity theft, contact the local Department of Motor Vehicles (DMV) in the state where your loved was licensed to drive and request your loved one's name be removed from the DMV's records. The DMV will require a copy of the death certificate and Letters of Administration or Letters Testamentary. As with all records, keep a copy of the canceled driver's license for your records.

Delete or Memorialize Social Media Accounts

In Chapter 8, we discussed digital assets such as social media. A social media provider will allow you, as the executor or personal representative, to delete your loved one's social media account. The provider also may give you the option of keeping the account online and switching it to a memorial or "remembering" profile. This is permitted by Twitter, Facebook, and Instagram but not TikTok. Whether you choose to delete or memorialize, you'll need to contact the providers with copies of the death certificate and Letters of Administration or Letters Testamentary. Remember that the provider's user agreement will specify how you can access, delete, and memorialize the account.

Delete Email Accounts

In Chapter 8, we also discussed obtaining access to your loved one's Yahoo, Gmail, Hotmail, and other email accounts. Emails, like regular mail received through the U.S. Postal Service, may provide information regarding your loved one's accounts, subscriptions, debts, assets and other items that need to be closed, paid, liquidated or otherwise handled. After you have reviewed your loved one's email accounts for any valuable information, you should close them to help prevent identity theft and fraud. Although the provider will likely require a copy of the death certificate and Letters of Administration or Letters Testamentary, the provider's user agreement will specify how you can access and delete the account.

Delete Voter Registration

Having your loved one's voter registration deleted is another step toward preventing identity theft. Depending on the state where your loved one is registered to vote, it may have a mechanism in place that automatically removes your loved one's name from voter registration rolls. If not, you will have to contact the state's office of the Secretary of State and notify it of your loved one's passing. It will require a copy of the death certificate and Letters of Administration or Letters Testamentary to remove your loved one's name from the voter registration roll.

Chapter Summary

In this chapter, you learned how to inform your loved one's employers, business partners, credit reporting agencies, the Social Security Administration, known and unknown creditors, insurance companies, utility companies, and others of your loved one's passing and how to request information regarding account balances, possible benefits, and other matters. You have accomplished a tremendous amount of work and moved your loved one's estate to its final stages.

In the next chapter, you'll learn what you need to do to pay your loved one's debts and taxes, distribute proceeds to heirs, and perform other tasks to close the estate.

Chapter 10

Paying Your Loved One's Debts and Taxes

C ongratulations! You've made it to the downhill portion of this long and exhausting, yet worthwhile, journey. In this chapter, you'll learn how to pay valid debts in order of priority, challenge questionable claims of creditors, negotiate debts, pay a variety of taxes, and obtain tax clearance and discharge of tax liability. Let's keep your momentum rolling toward the finish line!

Paying Valid Debts and Taxes—and Challenge Questionable Claims

Your previous investigation should have revealed most, if not all, of your loved one's debts and creditors. Other debtors also may have come forward after reading the public notice you provided in the newspaper. All your loved one's debts and creditors should be listed in the Debts and Expenses Paid Form you compiled.

Before providing heirs with any inheritance, your loved one's estate must pay all valid debts, including taxes. If there isn't enough cash on hand to pay all the creditors, then the executor typically sells a portion of the estate's assets necessary to pay the debts. As executor, you need to decide which assets will be sold and in what order. To some extent, the amount of cash that needs to be raised to pay remaining debts will dictate what assets may need to be sold. Use your best judgment and refer to the will and your Inventory List to review any assets your loved one may have bequeathed to specific heirs. Try to avoid selling these assets to pay debts if possible. If your loved one's assets aren't enough to pay all the debts, the creditor will be forced to write the debt off as unrecoverable. In this situation, the probate court will determine which creditors get paid and don't get paid.

As the executor, it's your responsibility to review the creditors' claims and determine their validity. Use your best judgment to decide whether it's an actual debt owed by your loved one or if it's a false claim. In rare circumstances, a creditor may make a claim for a debt against your loved one's estate without providing any proof of the alleged debt.

If you have any question regarding the debt's legitimacy, contact the creditor directly to discuss the claim and request proof of the debt. If the creditor can't provide you with proof of the debt and you still doubt its validity, inform the probate court that you're challenging a specific creditor's claim. Typically, this is done by filing a notice of disallowance of claim, or similar form, with the probate court. A sample Notice of Disallowance of Claim form can be accessed from my website, https://www.georgekoons.com/subscribe, after subscribing to my newsletter. Check with your local probate court to see if it has its own standard form applicable to disallowing clams. Ultimately, the probate judge will determine whether the debt is valid.

Once the validity of all debts has been determined, you pay the creditors of valid claims from the assets of your loved one's estate. However, don't pay any debts until the creditors claim period has ended and you have reviewed all the debts.

Pay Valid Debts in Order of Priority But Only When the Claim Period Has Ended

As part of the probate process, the probate court will order the deadline by which creditors must submit all claimed debts they have against your loved one's estate. Don't pay any debts until the period for debtors to submit claims has ended. That way, you can review all claims and determine their priority of payment. Claims against the estate must be paid according to the priority of the claim. Typically, the priority for payment of a claim is as follows: (1) federal income taxes, (2) burial and funeral claims, (3) general creditors, and (4) heirs. All higher priority claims must be paid in full before a lower priority claim can receive anything. Sometimes, the amount of the loved one's debts may exceed the amount of his or her assets. In this situation, potential heirs aren't liable for covering these debts, although this usually means there will be no assets left to distribute to heirs.

If the executor pays a lower priority claim before a higher priority claim has been fully paid, and the estate doesn't have enough money to pay the higher priority claim in full, then the executor may be held personally liable for the unpaid amount of the higher priority claim. To avoid this situation, wait until the claim period has ended, evaluate the priority of all claims, then pay the claims according to their priority. If there is a question about which claims have priority, or if your loved one's assets aren't enough to pay all the debts, advise the probate court of the situation and request its assistance in determining the creditor's priority for receiving payment from the estate.

Pay the Executor

If you're being compensated as the executor, now is the time to distribute the executor's compensation. In most states, paying the executor's compensation takes priority over paying general creditors but doesn't take priority over paying funeral expenses and taxes. If you're to receive compensation as your loved one's executor, make sure to check whether your compensation has priority over general creditors. If so, pay the executor prior to paying claims that have a lower priority.

In addition to compensation for services rendered on behalf of your loved one's estate, the executor is entitled to reimbursement from the estate for reasonable estate administration costs that were paid by the executor. These costs may include obtaining copies of the death certificate, notarization fees, certain payments made for expenses related to your loved one's estate, and other costs associated with managing the estate. You may not have any of these out-of-pocket costs if you established an estate banking account shortly after your loved one's passing. If you were able to do so and paid these costs directly from that account, then no reimbursement is necessary. You may be reimbursed for these estate expenses as they are incurred, although certain expenses may require prior approval from the probate court.

Negotiate Debts with Creditors When Possible

Although creditors don't have a duty to reduce your loved one's debt to them (if your loved one's estate has sufficient assets to pay the debt), it may be beneficial for them to do so. For instance, a smaller debt might not be worth the creditor's effort to collect the debt. When my mom died, she had several credit cards with balances under $1,000. When the credit card companies were told of her death, and that her estate had limited funds, two of the companies waived the balances completely. You may feel a bit like a used car salesman when negotiating these debts, but remember, you're doing this to help your loved one's estate. Any money you keep on the estate's side of the balance sheet benefits the heirs. So do what you can to reduce your loved one's debts.

To negotiate your loved one's debts, first review the debts, the balances currently owed on the accounts, and the priority of the debts. Don't negotiate settlement of a lower priority debt unless you know the estate has enough assets to cover the estate's higher priority debts. Next, determine the amount you're willing to pay to settle your loved one's debt with the creditor. Then call the creditor and let them know your loved one has passed away. Explain that you're the executor of your loved one's estate, the estate has limited assets, and you want to negotiate a settlement of the account. Typically, the initial customer service representative you speak with won't have the authority to negotiate a settlement and you'll be transferred to the "manager."

You'll likely need to provide the creditor with some motivation to entice it to reduce the debt and accept a lower amount than is owed. Depending on your situation, your loved one's estate may not have enough assets to cover all debts. It's in the creditor's best interest to settle the debt for a lower amount than is owed because the creditor won't incur the cost of participating in the probate process to seek its debt. This is especially true where debts are larger than assets and the creditor is unlikely to recover the full amount it's owed. By accepting a smaller amount than is owed with little effort, the creditor may recover at least a portion of the debt. Otherwise, it may find itself wasting time and resources in probate court with the possibility of recovering little. Also, the creditor may be entitled to write off the unrecoverable portion as a tax deduction. Given this scenario, it's in the creditor's best interests to quickly recover some of the debt with little effort.

In negotiating a debt settlement, your initial offer should be much lower than the amount owed. If the debt is $5,000, you might start with offering $800. Be strong with your offer. Instead of asking whether the creditor will accept $800 to settle the debt, explain that your loved one died with few assets and many bills. However, the estate has set aside $800 to settle your loved one's account with the creditor. Take a deep breath and let the creditor respond. If the creditor makes a counteroffer, pause in consideration, and increase your initial offer by a small amount. Reiterate that the assets aren't enough to cover the debts. If your loved one had a mortgage at the time of death, you may want to let the creditor know that a mortgage on the home has a priority lien and will be paid before the creditor's sub-priority debt. At some point, you need to stick with a final offer so the creditor understands the limited assets won't pay all the debts.

If the creditor agrees to an acceptable amount in exchange for the debt's settlement, ask the creditor to send you the offer in writing. Don't pay the offer until you receive the written agreement, the period for submitting claims has ended, and you've verified the payment will not be paid before higher priority debts are paid. After doing so, send the agreed upon payment via certified mail, return receipt requested, to ensure you have proof of delivery. Include a copy of the agreement along with the payment. As always, keep a record of your payment and copy of the agreement in a safe place in case the settlement or payment is disputed.

Selling Your Loved One's Assets

There are different reasons why the executor may want to sell assets of a loved one's estate. If your loved one's estate has more debts than cash on hand, then you may need to sell an asset or assets of the estate to pay these debts. Also, you may want to sell assets that are underperforming financially and invest the proceeds elsewhere. Further, as part of your asset disposition plan (discussed in Chapter 11), you may decide that selling the estate's assets is the easiest and most reasonable strategy for dividing up the estate and distributing it to heirs. Typically, distributing cash among heirs according to their residuary percentage is more straightforward than doling out motor vehicles, jewelry, real estate, and other similar assets. Of course, you need to distribute (not sell) any specific bequests to named beneficiaries per the terms of your loved one's will.

Methods to Sell Assets

Depending on the quantity and quality of the assets you intend to sell, you may decide to sell them yourself in a garage or estate sale. Unique or more valuable items such as jewelry, furniture, cars, or artwork may yield the highest return by selling them online or by contacting professionals or merchants familiar with these items. They may want to buy the items themselves or can recommend potential buyers. If there are many assets, it may be more efficient to have a professional auctioneer sell them in an auction. Professional auctions tend to attract more buyers, require less time, and may maximize your return even though the auction house usually earns a percentage of the sales. You can investigate auctions at www.auctioneer.org. Another selling option is an estate liquidator, which is similar to hiring an auction house. Investigate estate liquidators at www.estate sales.org.

Contact several of these professional sellers so you can compare services, pricing, and their backgrounds. They should have a written contract for you to sign detailing the process for selling your items, how the items will be priced, when the sale will be held and by what method, the price they will charge you for their service, and other issues. Like any contract, review it thoroughly and make sure you understand its terms before you sign it. If you have any questions or if the contract is unclear, discuss it with the seller and have any issue clarified in the contract before you sign it. Terms are almost always negotiable. Don't enter into a contract if it doesn't contain the terms that are important to you. Generally, having a written contract is good for all parties because it reduces the duties and expectations of the parties to writing and provides proof of each party's commitments. Just make sure you understand and agree to the contract's contents before signing it.

A Note About Firearms

Generally, the executor may sell firearms owned by the loved one to buyers or distribute firearms to heirs so long as it isn't illegal for the buyers or heirs to possess a firearm. However, certain firearms such as automatic weapons, silencers, and short-barreled rifles and shotguns may only be sold or distributed per the rules and regulations of the Bureau of Alcohol, Tobacco, Firearms and Explosives. Likewise, state law may have certain requirements related to the sale and possession of firearms. For instance, many states require the seller to perform a background check on a potential buyer. Other states may require firearms to be registered by anyone who possesses them. Usually, the executor has a short time to sell or distribute the loved one's firearms without having to personally register them. Then, it's up to the buyer or heir to register the firearm as required. When firearms are a part of your loved one's estate, be sure to check local and federal regulations about how they may be possessed, sold to a third party, or distributed to an heir.

Court Approval May Be Needed Before Selling Assets

Depending on the state where you opened probate, you may need the probate court's permission to sell your loved one's assets. Check with your probate court to verify whether you need such permission. If you do, contact your probate judge's clerk and ask how you make this request. It may require you to write a motion detailing the assets you'd like to sell and the reason for the sale. Don't sell any assets without the court's approval if required.

Evaluate, Calculate, and Pay Taxes

Depending on the value of your loved one's estate and the state where probate was filed, there may be a variety of tax forms the executor has to file with state and federal taxing authorities. In addition to taxes the estate may need to pay, your loved one's heirs may also have to pay taxes on their inheritance. The tax forms must be filed, and the taxes paid, by a certain deadline.

These taxes may include state and federal estate taxes, inheritance tax, property tax, and your loved one's personal income tax. Depending on the various taxes, forms, and deadlines involved with your loved one's estate, a good strategy for evaluating, calculating, and paying taxes involves hiring a certified tax professional to assist in the process. The following sections will give you a clearer picture of tax issues that may be involved with your loved one's estate and your need for a tax professional.

Estate and Inheritance Taxes

An estate tax is a tax on the net worth (value after debts have been paid) of your loved one's estate. Estate taxes may be due to state and federal taxing authorities. Any estate tax is applied to your loved one's estate before the assets are distributed to beneficiaries and is paid by your loved one's estate. The estate tax doesn't apply to assets that will be transferred to a surviving spouse.

An inheritance tax is a tax placed on the value of the portion of your loved one's estate inherited by a beneficiary. Any inheritance tax due is paid by the specific beneficiary, not the estate.

The amount of the exemptions related to estate and inheritance taxes often changes from year to year. Contact the IRS or a tax accountant for the current exemption amount.

Estate Taxes—Federal

Most estates aren't subject to a federal estate tax. If your loved one's estate is valued at less than $12.06 million (as of 2022) it enjoys a federal exemption and will not have to pay any federal estate tax. If the gross value of your loved one's estate exceeds $12.06 million, you will need to file a federal estate tax form (IRS Form 706) within nine months of your loved one's death and pay any estate tax. A six-month filing extension may be available under certain conditions. Even though you're required to file this form, it doesn't mean your loved one's estate will owe any taxes because taxes are calculated on the estate's net value. If your loved one's estate exceeds $12.06 million, you may want to request an "Estate Tax Closing Letter" from the IRS before you, as the executor, close the estate. However, you need to wait until six months after filing IRS Form 706 to request this closing letter. If your loved one has a large estate, you should hire a tax professional to confirm the likely issues, complications, and best course of action.

Even if your loved one's estate is exempt from paying a federal estate tax, it may be subject to a state estate tax. This is because state exemptions are much lower that the federal exemption. However, as of 2022, if your loved one's estate is valued at less than $1 million dollars, it will not be taxed by the IRS or any state taxing authority.

Estate Taxes—State

Estate taxes due to a state are determined by the state's law where the estate is being probated. The amount of estate tax varies greatly from state to state, with some states imposing a tax on the value of an estate that exceeds a specific, threshold amount. Only the amount that exceeds that threshold amount is subject to estate tax. Most states don't have an estate tax. As of 2022, only the following 12 states and the District of Columbia (Washington, D.C.) have an estate tax at the following rate:

Connecticut—11.6 to 12 percent if the net value of your loved one's estate is above $9.1 million

District of Columbia—11.2 to 16 percent if the net value of your loved one's estate is above $4.3 million

Hawaii—10 to 20 percent if the net value of your loved one's estate is above $5.5 million

Illinois—0.8 to 16 percent if the net value of your loved one's estate is above $4 million

Maine—8 to 12 percent if the net value of your loved one's estate is above $5.8 million

Maryland—0.8 to 16 percent if the net value of your loved one's estate is above $5 million

Massachusetts—0.8 to 16 percent if the net value of your loved one's estate is above $1 million

Minnesota—13 to 16 percent if the net value of your loved one's estate is above $3 million

New York—3.06 to 16 percent if the net value of your loved one's estate is above $6.1 million

Oregon—10 to 16 percent if the net value of your loved one's estate is above $1 million

Rhode Island—0.8 to 16 percent if the net value of your loved one's estate is above $1.7 million

Vermont—16 percent if the net value of your loved one's estate is above $5 million

Washington—10 to 20 percent if the net value of your loved one's estate is above $2.2 million

The states that have estate taxes change from time to time, as do the tax rates. Verify whether the state where your loved one's estate is being probated has an estate tax and, if it does, the tax rate.

Inheritance Tax—State Only

The good news is there is no federal inheritance tax. However, your loved one's beneficiaries may be liable for state inheritance taxes. An inheritance tax is a tax placed on the value of the portion of your loved one's estate inherited by the individual beneficiary. An inheritance tax is paid by the beneficiary, not by your loved one's estate, in accordance with the law of the state where your loved one resided at the time of his or her death. As of 2022, only Iowa, Kentucky, Maryland, Nebraska, New Jersey, and Pennsylvania have an inheritance tax, as follows:

Iowa—up to 9 percent of inheritance

Kentucky—up to 16 percent of inheritance

Maryland—up to 10 percent of inheritance

Nebraska—up to 18 percent of inheritance

New Jersey—up to 16 percent of inheritance

Pennsylvania—up to 15 percent of inheritance

If your loved one didn't reside in one of these states at the time of death, then the beneficiaries won't have to pay an inheritance tax. The states that have inheritance taxes change from time to time, so verify whether the state where your loved one resided at passing has an inheritance tax.

Personal Income Taxes

If your loved one earned more than the minimum amount of income, as set by federal and state law, during the year of his or her death, then the executor needs to file final personal income tax forms for the loved one. These are typically due by the U.S. income tax deadline of April 15 of the calendar year following your loved one's death. You're also responsible for filing tax returns for any previous years that your loved one was required to file returns but didn't do so. Depending on the date your loved one passed away, there may be little time to meet the filing deadline. To avoid a penalty for filing late, you may be able to file for an extension of the filing deadline. Your loved one's final income tax filing may be done as a joint return if he or she is survived by a spouse who hasn't remarried. If your loved one already filed personal income tax returns for a previous year and a refund is due, you can collect it by filing IRS Form 1310 for the appropriate year.

Real Property Taxes

If your loved one's estate includes real property, the executor must pay any associated annual real property taxes until the property is sold or distributed to heirs. Depending on the state, these property taxes may be due twice a year.

Obtain Tax Clearances

Once you've filed all state and federal tax returns and paid all taxes associated with your loved one's estate, request and obtain releases from the IRS and the state taxing authority. These releases prove that all estate related tax liabilities have been fulfilled. The probate court may also require you to file these releases with the court before the probate judge will officially close your loved one's estate.

Discharging Tax Liability

Typically, the IRS has three years from the date a tax return is submitted to analyze the return, determine if there is any deficiency in the amount of taxes paid, and request payment of the deficiency. If all taxes related to your loved one's estate weren't paid in full, you, the executor, may be held personally liable for the unpaid taxes. You can reduce the period the IRS has to review the estate's returns and request any tax deficiency from three years to nine months (six months in some cases). You do this by filing IRS Form 5495 after all other required tax forms related to your loved one's estate have been filed.

Filing Form 5495 isn't mandatory. However, reducing the IRS's response time by 27 months is helpful because you'll find out quicker if there is a tax deficiency. If there is a tax deficiency, you may be able to timely resolve it with funds from the estate before making distributions to beneficiaries. Technically, you aren't required to wait the nine months after filing Form 5495 to distribute your loved one's estate to the beneficiaries. Nevertheless, you may be held personally responsible for any tax deficiency if the estate doesn't have enough funds to pay the deficiency due to your distribution of funds to beneficiaries.

Chapter Summary

In this chapter, you learned how to challenge questionable claims against your loved one's estate, negotiate debts when possible, and pay valid debts after the claim period has ended. You also learned how to evaluate, calculate, and pay estate, inheritance, real property, and personal taxes; obtain tax clearances; and discharge your tax liability. It certainly wasn't easy, but performing these time-consuming and stressful tasks has brought you to the point where you'll begin distributing your loved one's assets. This will be one of your more rewarding duties, and I'll show you how to get it done in Chapter 11.

Chapter 11

Create an Asset Disposition Plan and Distribute Assets to Heirs

Now that your loved one's creditors, debts, and taxes have been paid, it's time for you, as the executor, to dispose of the remainder of your loved one's assets, perform a final accounting, and obtain approval of the accounting from the probate court. Note that some probate courts require the final accounting be performed before distributing the loved one's remaining assets to heirs; other probate courts require an accounting after the distribution to heirs has been made. Check with the probate court where you opened probate for its accounting requirements before distributing any remaining assets to heirs. If the final accounting is required before distributing the remaining assets to heirs, then review Chapter 12 and perform the final accounting prior to distributing assets.

Distribute Your Loved One's Remaining Assets—But First Make a Plan

As the executor, distributing your loved one's assets to beneficiaries is usually one of the last tasks you perform. Distributing assets last gives you the opportunity to verify assets and debts, pay creditors and various taxes, obtain tax clearance, and discharge tax liability. However, before distributing assets, you need to make a plan called an "asset disposition plan." Taking the time to create a plan will make the actual distribution of assets straightforward. For the most part, you'll simply follow your plan.

Automatic Transfers to Named Beneficiaries—a Reminder

As previously discussed in Chapter 6, certain transfers to beneficiaries may happen automatically outside the control of the estate. These automatic transfers may include bank accounts, investment accounts, mortgage loans, life insurance policies, and other assets that have a named beneficiary. In these situations, the loved one's account is automatically transferred to the named beneficiary without the need for a designation of the transfer in the will. Depending on the law of the state where you filed probate, automatic transfers likely receive "priority" and will occur before any other assets of the estate are distributed to heirs. So, any automatic transfers to your loved one's named beneficiaries will not be considered in your asset disposition plan because they automatically occurred upon your loved one's death.

Create an Asset Disposition Plan

Your goal as executor is to carry out your loved one's intent as provided in the will, while satisfying your legal obligations as executor. Your asset disposition plan will help you accomplish this goal. The plan is your blueprint for distributing your loved one's assets, treating similar situations in a consistent manner, and handling the competing interest of heirs.

As previously discussed, the executor must satisfy all debts before distributing the loved one's assets to heirs. Therefore, we're starting with the presumption that all your loved one's debts have been paid as outlined in Chapter 10, including selling certain assets as needed to satisfy these debts. After resolving these debts, your goal is to distribute 100% of the remaining value of your loved one's estate, with each heir receiving the proper items and the correct overall share of the estate as set forth in the will.

Specific Items Designated for Named Beneficiaries

Your asset disposition plan will be guided by the terms of the will, which may bequeath certain personal possessions and assets, called "bequests," to specific heirs, called "named beneficiaries." In Chapter 8, you uncovered your loved one's assets and personal possessions; completed an Inventory List recording these assets and possessions; and noted which assets and possessions, if any, were left to a specific heir per the terms of the will. Taking care of these bequests first is a good way to begin asset disposition. However, there are situations when not all your loved one's bequests can be honored.

Certain items that were designated for specific heirs may have been lost, destroyed, or irretrievably given away prior to your loved one's death. If so, these items are technically no longer part of your loved one's estate and can't be bequeathed. Likewise, you may have had to sell an asset that your loved one intended to be bequeathed as a last resort to pay the debts of the estate. Sometimes, a bequest of an item as stated in the will conflicts with local law, such as in a community property state where the property is owned in common by husband and wife (discussed in Chapter 8).

When bequests can no longer be honored, they are reduced or eliminated. The process of reducing bequests is called "abatement." Depending on the state's law where you filed probate, an abatement is typically proportional. For example, if the estate is worth $100,000 and there are two bequests totaling $100,000, both bequests would be reduced by 50 percent or by $50,000 each. Each heir would receive $50,000. In another example, if the will bequeathed a diamond broach to an heir but the broach was lost prior to the loved one's death, then the bequest would go unfulfilled, and the heir wouldn't receive the broach. Even if the estate has money left over after paying all its debts, the executor typically isn't permitted to use estate funds to compensate the heir for the value of the object that wasn't bequeathed—in this case a diamond broach.

After you make the specific distributions to the named beneficiaries as stated in your loved one's will, you need to decide your strategy for handling the remainder of the estate's assets and personal possessions.

Selling Assets to Raise Cash to Distribute to Heirs

Depending on the will and the contents of your loved one's estate, you may want to sell the remainder of the assets to raise as much cash as possible and distribute it according to the heirs' percentage of inheritance as stated in the will. You may decide to sell them yourself or hire a company that will hold an estate sale and keep a percentage of the sale's proceeds. Selling your loved one's assets was discussed in Chapter 10.

Selling the remainder of the assets makes distributing the estate to the heirs easier, as you're just distributing cash. Of course, these assets should be capable of being sold relatively quickly at a fair market value. When the assets are sold you simply divide the total amount of the estate by the percentage of inheritance each heir has been given under the terms of the will. For instance, if your loved one's estate totals $100,000 after all assets have been sold and the will says that each of four heirs receives an equal one-quarter share, then each heir receives $25,000.

Undesignated Items an Heir Requests—Offsets

Sometimes, there are valuable, meaningful assets an heir would like, such as expensive jewelry, artwork, a collector car, or other objects, that weren't specifically left to the heir. To satisfy an heir's request for such items, you may determine the fair market value of the items and deduct that amount from the heir's total inheritance. Valuing your loved one's assets was discussed on Chapter 8. For example, let's suppose that one of four heirs wants a car with a fair market value of $20,000. You've determined that the total value of the estate is $100,000, and each of the four heirs receives an equal inheritance of $25,000. Subtracting the $20,000 value of the car from the individual heir's total inheritance leaves that heir with $5,000 in addition to the car. When reasonable, try to find ways to accommodate specific requests of "unnamed" beneficiaries.

Personal Possessions

Your asset disposition plan should also consider what to do with your loved one's personal possessions. If your loved one's estate is anything like my parents' estate, there will be many personal possessions. Some may have great meaning, and you want to keep them in the family. Others may not be worth a lot of money, can't be sold easily, and aren't worth keeping. Start by determining which personal possessions are meaningful and will be kept by the heirs. Next, determine which possessions are worth selling—maybe at a garage or estate sale. Lastly, decide which items will be donated to a charity, given away, or thrown away.

Distributing your loved one's personal possessions among heirs usually isn't a problem unless multiple heirs want the same item. In that case, you need to figure out a system that fairly allocates your loved one's personal possession to the heirs. When my parents died, they had many interesting personal items that had meaning to me and each of my four brothers and sisters. We agreed to group these items by their estimated intrinsic value and draw straws to determine everyone's "picking order." Although we didn't always get the item we wanted, we were able to pick other items that were important to us. I ended up trading several items with other siblings to get objects that had more significance to me. Although this was an unscientific process, we all behaved like adults, and it achieved its purpose to divvy up personal items that didn't have much monetary value.

Be careful not to sell or donate personal items you may later wish you had kept. The opposite is also true. Although you may feel the responsibility to keep many items that are unique to your loved one, take a few minutes to envision what you'll do with these items. When my dad died, I saved a lot of his interior design and architectural drawings as well as some furniture. I kept them in a storage unit for over a year. Looking back, I think I did this out of a sense of loyalty even though I had no idea what to do with everything. I ended up framing some of his drawings but throwing most of the items away. Rather than feeling guilty for doing so, I felt relieved. I realized my dad didn't expect me to be the keeper of his life's possessions.

If your loved one's will provides for charitable donations, distribute these donations to charities in the same manner you'd distribute assets to any other heir. Even if the will didn't specifically provide for charitable donations, there may be items that none of the heirs want and should be donated. In this situation, it's a good idea to draft a document listing the items to be donated, the charity receiving the donation, and approval of the donations by the heirs. You can estimate the value of the donations, divide the value by the number of heirs, and make the donation in the name of the heirs. The donations may be a tax deduction for the heirs.

Have the Heirs Sign Receipts for Distributions Received

It's a good practice to require all heirs to sign a receipt for distributions they received. The receipt may simply list the heir's name, the date he or she received the asset, and a thorough description of the specific asset received. The receipt should be signed and dated by the heir. The receipt may list multiple items, or you may have several receipts for several items. The idea is to document all distributions to heirs and have them acknowledge their receipt of the items.

Having each heir acknowledge receipt of assets is useful if a conflict arises regarding receipt of an item. As usual, keep the receipts in a safe place with other records related to your loved one's estate. Similarly, you should keep track of the assets you distribute. Use the Inventory List to check off under "beneficiary" when an item has been distributed.

A Sample Asset Disposition Plan

Depending on your loved one's estate, the terms of the will, and your personal asset disposition plan, distributing assets (after all debts have been satisfied) may be best done in the following order:

1. Distribute specific assets and personal possessions to named beneficiaries (specific heirs) as stated in the will.

2. Distribute specific assets to heirs who want them, in lieu of being sold, in exchange for a reduction of that heir's inheritance by the fair market value of the specific asset.

3. Sell remaining assets at fair market value to raise cash to distribute to heirs per the will.

4. Distribute cash to heirs according to their percentage of inheritance as stated in the will.

5. Distribute personal possession among heirs.

6. Sell, donate, or throw away remaining possessions.

Of course, this sample asset disposition plan may be adjusted to meet your specific needs and circumstances.

Distributing Assets When Your Loved Died Without a Will

If your loved passed away without a will (died intestate), your loved one's remaining assets will be transferred to beneficiaries according to the intestacy laws of the state where probate was filed. Generally, your loved one's heirs will inherit property depending on their degree of kinship. This topic was discussed in Chapters 4 and 6.

Chapter Summary

In this chapter, you learned how to create an asset disposition plan that best suits your situation and distribute the remainder of your loved one's assets. Your selfless mission is almost over. In the next, and final, chapter, you'll learn how to perform a final accounting of your loved one's estate, tie up loose ends, and close the estate.

Chapter 12

Perform a Final Accounting and Close Your Loved One's Estate

You've ridden the emotional roller coaster, endured sleepless nights, and performed a lot of hard work on behalf of your loved one to get to this stage. Well done! Now, it's time to wrap things up, perform a final accounting, and close your loved one's estate.

Perform the Final Accounting of Your Loved One's Estate

The final accounting summarizes financial dealings related to your loved one's estate that occurred after your loved one's death. It shows the assets of your loved one's estate at the time of death, all additions and subtractions to and from the estate, and the ending assets distributed to the beneficiaries. The executor typically files the final accounting form with the probate court for approval after all valid claims have been paid, the claim period has ended, and the remaining assets have been distributed to heirs. A sample Final (or Interim) Accounting Form illustrating what's typically included in a final accounting can be accessed on my website, https://www.georgekoons.com/subscribe, after signing up for my newsletter. Some probate courts require an accounting before the loved one's remaining assets are distributed to heirs; other probate courts require an accounting after the distribution to heirs has been made. Check with the probate court where you opened probate for its accounting requirements.

Depending on your specific probate court, the final accounting includes the following: (1) an inventory of your loved one's assets; (2) assets that were sold and the corresponding amount of their sale; (3) the total amount of funds received on behalf of your loved one; and (4) total expenses and disbursements made on behalf of the estate, including the distributions to heirs and any compensation to the executor. The executor performs the final accounting by reviewing the activities related to the assets, income, and expenses of the loved one's estate; completing the final accounting form; and filing the form with the probate court for approval. Many probate courts have approved "final accounting" forms, so check with your probate court for its form.

Obtain Approval of the Final Accounting from the Probate Court

The goal of submitting the final accounting form to the probate court is to obtain the court's approval of the final accounting— approval of the financial activities related to your loved one's estate. Typically, the probate court will hold a hearing on the final accounting with the executor and heirs. However, if all the heirs accept the final accounting, the probate court may waive the final accounting hearing. To request waiver of the hearing, you must file the final accounting form with an "acceptance of accounting and waiver of a formal hearing" form, or similar form, that has been signed by all the heirs. Again, check with your probate court for the form it uses. Complete the form with the applicable information related to your loved one's estate and file it with the probate court.

When you provide the acceptance of accounting and waiver of a formal hearing form to your loved one's heirs for signing, give them a tight deadline for returning the signed form to you. After you receive the signed form from all the heirs, file it, and the final accounting form, with your probate court. The court will likely approve the final accounting without holding a formal hearing because all the heirs have accepted the final accounting and waived the hearing. If you can't obtain the signatures from all your loved one's heirs accepting the final accounting, the probate court will hold a formal hearing on the final accounting. This hearing provides the heirs with the opportunity to object to the accounting.

File a Closing Statement with the Court, Obtain Approval, and Close the Estate

Your loved one's probate case is ready to be closed after all the estate's assets are transferred out of your loved one's name, applicable tax returns are filed and paid, all legitimate claims of creditors are satisfied, and the remaining assets have been distributed to beneficiaries according to the will. If the estate's bank account is still open, now is the time to close it.

You must prepare a closing statement or closing affidavit declaring that you, as executor, have resolved all the estate's debts, paid all taxes dues, and distributed the estate's net proceeds appropriately. The form of the closing statement varies among the various probate courts, so check with your applicable probate court for the closing statement it prefers. Some closing statements may be in the form of an affidavit, meaning the executor needs to sign it under oath in front of a notary public, who will stamp and sign the affidavit. The last step is to file the completed closing statement (signed and notarized as may be required) with the probate court for its approval. Once the court approves the closing statement, your loved one's probate case will be officially closed.

File Final Form 56 with the IRS

If you filed a Form 56 with the IRS as the executor (discussed in Chapter 8), you should now file a corresponding Form 56 with the IRS. The form notifies the IRS that you have completed your duties as executor and terminated your responsibilities.

Final Words

Making it to the point of finalizing and closing your loved one's estate results in a feeling that is truly beyond words. Not only have you dealt with the loss of your loved one, you've endured countless obstacles, emotions, road blocks, issues, confrontations, and hours spent finalizing your loved one's last wishes and cleaning up related messes. Maybe not now, but at some point, you will experience a sense of well-deserved satisfaction. You have performed a true act of love, respect, and kindness for which you will be proud of the rest of your life. As I said in the beginning of this journey, your loved one chose you to do this because he or she knew you'd get it done. Congratulations!

PLEASE LEAVE A REVIEW!

If you enjoyed this book and found it helpful, I would be very grateful if you would leave a brief review with Amazon. Reviews will help me gain visibility and traction as a new author and bring my books to the attention of other readers in need.

To leave a review, sign in to your Amazon account, go to Accounts & Lists, Your Account, Orders, and Write a product review. Or you can open Amazon on your web browser, find the book, scroll down to Customer reviews, and Review this product.

Thank you!

—*George*

JOIN THE TEAM & SUBSCRIBE TO MY NEWSLETTER

Hey there! If you would like to get helpful information related to topics in my book, sign up for my newsletter. You will have access to the Team section of my website where you'll find useful sample forms, letters, pleadings, and other documents, and hear about my newest books before anyone else. It's completely free to sign up and you will never be spammed by me or inundated with emails. You can opt out easily at any time. Sign up at https://www.georgekoons.com/subscribe.

—George

About the Author

George Koons is the principal and owner of Koons Law Group Ltd. For the past twenty-five years George has specialized in defending complex product liability lawsuits for motor vehicle manufacturers. When his mother died, he found he wasn't ready or able to deal with the loss – practicably or legally. Like many people in his situation, he was lost in the unfamiliar world of coping with a loved one's death while trying to accomplish the many practical and legal tasks that would not wait for his grief to end. With the intent of making the loss of a loved one easier on others, he decided to use his newly gained knowledge and legal expertise to simplify the many practical and legal issues which accompany a loved one's death. This guide is the result of his exploration and findings, distilled to the point of common understanding to be used by a loved one or executor.

Much of George's time is now spent helping people overcome life's obstacles by providing easy to understand, step-by-step practical and legal guidance through the power of books. He's a new author who plans to use the digital revolution to enrich people's lives, empower their decision making, and level the playing field.

George earned a bachelor's degree in business administration from the University of Northern Colorado and a Juris Doctor degree from Whittier College School of Law in California. He was awarded the American Jurisprudence Award for Advanced Legal Writing and is the recipient of the Outstanding Young Lawyer Award and the

American Bar Association's Military Pro Bono Project Outstanding Services Award.

George served in the U.S. Marine Corps, Second Marine Air Wing, and currently provides pro bono work for active military members and their families. He is married and the father of three boys. George lives in the Colorado mountains, where he can often be found hiking, biking, skiing, and exploring.

Appendix

- Glossary
- Executor's Checklist
- Inventory List
- Debt and Expenses Paid Form (*sample*)
- Notice of Death to Bank (*sample*)
- Notice of Death to Credit Card Companies (*sample*)
- Notice of Death to Utility Companies (*sample*)
- Notice of Death to Credit Reporting Agency (*sample*)
- Notice of Death to Mortgage Lender (*sample*)
- Notice of Death to Pension Provider (*sample*)

The above glossary, checklists, forms, sample letters, and other helpful documents, are also available at my website, https://www.georgekoons.com, once you subscribe to my newsletter.

***PLEASE NOTE**: The above sample notices are only samples. They are provided to give you an example of the contents of certain notices.*

SAMPLE COURT FORMS*: **Sample court forms and pleadings typically used in a probate case may be found on my website, <u>https://www.georgekoons.com</u>. Subscribing to the newsletter and joining the Team will give you access to these sample forms, pleadings, and other materials. The purpose of these documents is to give you an idea of the information that a typical form or pleading may include in its contents. Do not rely upon these samples for your matter. They are not specific to your loved one, the estate, or your situation. Probate courts have different rules and requirements depending on the state. Court forms that you intend to use in your matter should be obtained from the probate court applicable to your matter or a local probate attorney. Many courts provide these forms, and instructions for completing the forms, free of charge on their website or at the courthouse.***

Glossary

Simplifying Complicated Legal Terms

Abatement: The process of reducing a specific bequest or asset that your loved one intended for a beneficiary. Certain bequests may need to be abated or reduced because the asset is no longer part of the estate, the bequest conflicts with local law such as the local community property law, or the bequest must be sold to pay estate debts.

Administrator: A person appointed by the probate court to manage or take charge of the assets and liabilities of the decedent (the deceased, your loved one). The administrator is similar to the executor. The main difference is that the court-appointed person is called the "administrator" when the loved one passed away without a will. If the loved one had a will, then the person was appointed by your loved in the will and is referred to as the "executor," or possibly the "executrix" if the person is female, or personal representative.

Assets: All of the property and other resources owned by a person (your loved one) that have some value. After your loved one passes, his or her assets will be used to pay the debts (also referred to as "liabilities"). Any assets remaining after his or her debts are paid are distributed to his or her heirs.

Affidavit: A sworn, written statement signed by a person under oath and before a notary public. The person signing the statement is called the "affiant."

Beneficiary: A person who benefits from the act of another, such as a person named in your loved one's will who receives specific property. In addition to a beneficiary of a will, a person may be a beneficiary of a trust, life insurance policy, financial account, or estate.

Bequest; bequeath: The act of leaving property, usually personal property, by a will to a beneficiary or heir. When used as a noun, bequest refers to the property itself.

Codicil: A document that changes the existing will in any way. A codicil is a separate legal document from the will and is also known as an "amendment" to a will. A codicil may explain, confirm, or change (either add to or subtract from) the existing will. Typically, a codicil is used to make fairly minor changes to a will without having to draft a new will. For example, one may use a codicil to change the executor, add a new asset, or change a beneficiary (such as removing an ex-husband).

Creditor: A person or company to whom your loved one owes money.

Decedent: The person who died, your loved one.

Devise: Property that is transferred under the terms of a will.

Devisee: The person to whom land or real property is devised or given under the terms of a will.

Estate: The property that your loved one, the decedent, owns or has an ownership interest in at the time of his or her death. The estate is administered or overseen by the executor.

Executor or Executrix: The person appointed by your loved one's will to carry out your loved one's requests after his or her death. This person also may be known as the "personal representative" of your loved one's estate. The executor is legally responsible for determining your loved one's finances, debts and expenses, paying those debts, and distributing the remainder of your loved one's property to the heirs per the terms of the will. The executor has a duty to act fairly, impartially, and in an expedient manner. Typically, the executor is a family member, close friend, or attorney. If the person is female, she may be referred to as the "executrix." An executor or executrix is similar to the administrator but has been appointed by the loved one's will, not the probate court, to administer the estate.

Heir: A person who would inherit property through a will or from someone who died without leaving a will.

Intestate: If your loved one died <u>without</u> a will, he or she is said to have died "intestate."

Joint Tenancy: Property that is held equally by two or more parties, the share of each passing to the other or others on death.

Legatee: A person named in your loved one's will to receive property. A legatee is also called a "beneficiary" and is similar to an heir.

Letters of Administration: The formal documents issued by the probate court, when your loved one passed away *without* a will, appointing a person as the administrator of your loved one's estate.

Letters Testamentary: The formal documents issued by the probate court, when your loved one passed away *with* a will, appointing the executor and giving the executor the authority to perform his or her duties as executor (e.g., pay bills, file tax returns, manage and distribute assets, open and close bank accounts, etc.). Letters testamentary, which are sometimes called "surrogate certificates," are the equivalent of letters of administration granted to an administrator when the loved one died without a will (intestate).

Liabilities: Money or debts owed to another.

Living Will: A living will is a written document outlining the medical treatment a person (your loved one) wants to receive when they can no longer express their wishes or give their medical consent for their own treatment. A living will is sometimes referred to as a health care declaration, advance directive, or advanced medical directive. Don't let the word "will" in living will confuse you. A living will isn't a last will and testament and isn't used to leave property or name an executor or a guardian.

Personal Representative: The person who manages and directs the administration of the estate of another person, such as your loved one's estate. Sometimes the term "executor" is used interchangeably with "personal representative."

Petition for Probate: A legal document filed with the probate court to begin the probate process. It's typically filed by the executor to admit the will to probate and appoint the executer or, if there is no will, to appoint a person who will administer the estate.

Probate: The legal process of reviewing the will, determining whether it's legal, and administering the estate according to the terms of the will. Your loved one's estate may be subject to probate whether he or she died with or without a will.

Probate Court: The court that handles your loved one's estate and probate.

Probate Estate: All of the assets your loved one owned when he or she died that will need a legal proceeding, such as probate, to transfer title of your loved one's assets to his or her heirs.

Property: Property includes both real property and personal property.

Personal Property: Anything that isn't real property, including cash, bank accounts, stocks, mutual funds, retirement accounts, motor vehicles, and personal effects.

Real Property: Real estate, including the land and any crops or structures on the land.

Residuary Estate: The amount or value of the estate remaining after all debts have been paid and any specific bequests have been distributed.

Residuary Percentage: The percentage of the residuary estate which the heir is entitled to receive per the terms of the Will.

Successor: Persons other than creditors who are entitled to property of your deceased loved one under a will or by a statute (e.g., your loved one's spouse or children).

Testate: When a person dies *with* a valid will. Testate is the opposite of intestate.

Testator: The person who makes a valid will (your loved one).

Title Company: A company that certifies that the title to a piece of real property is legitimate.

Title Insurance: Insurance issued by a title insurance company that protects the lender and/or owner against lawsuits or claims against the property resulting from disputes over the property's title.

Will (Last Will and Testament): A legal document that takes effect after your loved one's death and details his or her requests as well as how the real and personal property are to be disposed. There are different types of wills, such as self-proving wills and holographic wills. The will also may be referred to as the "Last Will and Testament," although it's referred to throughout this book simply as the "will."

Self-Proving Will: A will that includes an affidavit or sworn statement signed by a witness under the penalty of perjury. A self-proving will may be admitted to probate without the testimony of the witness.

Holographic Will: A will that is completely handwritten, dated, and signed by the person making the will. Although a holographic will may be considered a simple form of a will, it has full legal effect unless it's shown not to be genuine.

Executor's Checklist

Use this checklist to guide you through the process of settling your loved one's estate.

- Find the will and identify the executor of your loved one's estate
- Confirm the cause of death
- Arrange to have your loved one's body transferred
- Keep tabs on your emotions and health
- Reach out to family and friends
- Write the obituary
- Plan the funeral and have your loved one's body prepared
- Obtain certified copies of the death certificate
- Determine your loved one's beneficiaries
- Evaluate the need for professional help - select and hire an attorney to assist the executor.
- Pay attention to deadlines and important documents as you come across them
- Determine whether to open a formal or informal estate (probate)

- Open probate and lodge/submit the will with the probate court
- Discover and inventory your loved one's assets
- Value your loved one's assets
- Investigate the rights of a surviving spouse – family entitlements
- Protect your loved one's assets
- Obtain an EIN for your loved one's estate from the IRS
- Open a bank account for your loved one's estate
- File Form 56 with the IRS
- Protect your loved one's identity
- Determine your loved one's debts and creditors
- Determine notification requirements; notify social security, insurance companies, creditors, and others
- Protect your loved one's identity – cancel passport and driver's license, delete email accounts and voter registration, delete, or memorialize social media accounts
- Challenge questionable debts and claims of creditors
- Pay valid debts in order of priority – BUT only when the claim period has ended
- Negotiate debts with creditors when possible
- Sell your loved one's assets if necessary to pay creditors
- Evaluate, calculate, and pay any federal and state estate, real estate, and inheritance taxes
- Obtain tax clearance and discharge tax liability
- Distribute your loved one's assets after making an asset disposition plan
- Perform a final accounting of your loved one's estate, file it with the court, obtain approval
- File a closing statement with the court and obtain approval
- Close your loved one's estate
- File final Form 56 with the IRS

Inventory List

Use this Inventory List to record your loved one's assets, with a description, location, beneficiary entitled to the asset (if known), and value of each asset. Note whether any lien, tax or other "obstacle," including a loan, encumbers or restricts ownership of the asset. You can use the completed Inventory List to fill out a formal inventory form or final accounting that may be required by your probate court. It will also keep you organized and simplify the inventory process. The Inventory List and other helpful documents are also available at my website, https://www.georgekoons.com, once you subscribe to my newsletter.

REAL ESTATE
Description
Location
Beneficiary
Value
Lien/Loan/Obstacle

MORTGAGE/LENDER

Description
Location
Beneficiary
Value
Lien/Loan/Obstacle

INVESTMENT ACCOUNTS*
Description/Account No.
Location
Beneficiary
Value
Lien/Loan/Obstacle

INVESTMENT ACCOUNTS*
Description/Account No.
Location
Beneficiary
Value
Lien/Loan/Obstacle

INVESTMENT ACCOUNTS*
Description/Account No.
Location
Beneficiary
Value
Lien/Loan/Obstacle

INVESTMENT ACCOUNTS*
Description/Account No.
Location
Beneficiary
Value
Lien/Loan/Obstacle

NOTES
Description
Location
Beneficiary
Value
Lien/Loan/Obstacle

CASH
Description
Location
Beneficiary
Value
Lien/Loan/Obstacle

BANK ACCOUNTS - CHECKING
Description/Account No.
Location
Beneficiary
Value
Loans?

BANK ACCOUNTS - CHECKING
Description/Account No.
Location
Beneficiary
Value
Lien/Loan/Obstacle

BANK ACCOUNTS - SAVING
Description/Account No.
Location
Beneficiary
Value

Lien/Loan/Obstacle

BANK ACCOUNTS - SAVING
>   **Description/Account No.**
>   **Location**
>   **Beneficiary**
>   **Value**
>   **Lien/Loan/Obstacle**

CERTIFICATES OF DEPOSIT
>   **Description**
>   **Location**
>   **Beneficiary**
>   **Value**
>   **Lien/Loan/Obstacle**

HEALTH SAVINGS ACCOUNT
>   **Description**
>   **Location**
>   **Beneficiary**
>   **Value**
>   **Lien/Loan/Obstacle**

LIFE INSURANCE
>   **Description**
>   **Location**
>   **Beneficiary**
>   **Value**
>   **Lien/Loan/Obstacle**

OTHER INSURANCE
>   **Description**
>   **Location**

Beneficiary
Value
Lien/Loan/Obstacle

OTHER INSURANCE
   Description
   Location
   Beneficiary
   Value
   Lien/Loan/Obstacle

RETIREMENT FUNDS**
   Description/Account No.
   Location
   Beneficiary
   Value
   Lien/Loan/Obstacle

RETIREMENT FUNDS**
   Description/Account No.
   Location
   Beneficiary
   Value
   Lien/Loan/Obstacle

RETIREMENT FUNDS**
   Description/Account No.
   Location
   Beneficiary
   Value
   Lien/Loan/Obstacle

MOTOR/RECREATIONAL/OTHER VEHICLES

Description/VIN
Location
Beneficiary
Value
Lien/Loan/Obstacle

MOTOR/RECREATIONAL/OTHER VEHICLES
Description/VIN
Location
Beneficiary
Value
Lien/Loan/Obstacle

OTHER ASSETS
Description
Location
Beneficiary
Value
Lien/Loan/Obstacle

OTHER ASSETS
Description
Location
Beneficiary
Value
Lien/Loan/Obstacle

OTHER ASSETS
Description
Location
Beneficiary
Value
Lien/Loan/Obstacle

OTHER ASSETS
Description
Location
Beneficiary
Value
Lien/Loan/Obstacle

OTHER ASSETS
Description
Location
Beneficiary
Value
Lien/Loan/Obstacle

Investment Accounts include stocks, bonds, mutual funds, securities, cryptocurrencies, and other investment accounts.

**Retirement Funds include pensions, profit sharing plans, annuities, and other retirement funds.

Debt And Expenses Paid Form

Use the information you uncover to prepare a list of your loved one's debts, names of creditors, type of debt owed to the creditor (credit card, mortgage, utility, etc.), balance, payment amount, due date, and the amount and date paid. The Debt and Expenses Paid Form, and other helpful documents, are also available at my website, https://www.georgekoons.com. once you subscribe to my newsletter.

Creditor
  Type of Debt
  Account Number
  Balance
  Payment Amount
  Due Date
  Date Paid

Creditor
  Type of Debt
  Account Number

Balance
Payment Amount
Due Date
Date Paid

Creditor
    Type of Debt
    Account Number
    Balance
    Payment Amount
    Due Date
    Date Paid

Creditor
    Type of Debt
    Account Number
    Balance
    Payment Amount
    Due Date
    Date Paid

Creditor
    Type of Debt
    Account Number
    Balance
    Payment Amount
    Due Date
    Date Paid

Creditor
    Type of Debt
    Account Number
    Balance

Payment Amount
Due Date
Date Paid

Creditor
Type of Debt
Account Number
Balance
Payment Amount
Due Date
Date Paid

Sample Notice Of Death – Bank/Financial Institution

[Your name]
[Address line 1]
[Address line 2]
[Telephone No.]
[E-mail address]

[Date]

[Name of Bank or Financial Institution]
[Address line 1]
[Address line 2]

Re: [name of deceased], Notice of Death and Request for Information

Account number(s) [account number(s)]

To Whom It May Concern:

I am the executor of the estate of [deceased] who died on [date]. Please find enclosed a copy of the death certificate and a copy of the legal document proving my authority as the deceased's executor.

Please inform me of the following as soon as possible:

- The current balance on the account(s) and the balance on the date of the deceased's death.
- The amount of interest paid during the current tax year up to the date of death and the amount of any tax deducted.
- Details of any outstanding direct debits, standing orders, or otherwise, which I will instruct you on once received.
- Any other accounts, loans, safety deposit boxes, or otherwise that the deceased has with your institution or affiliates.

Please do not hesitate to contact me to discuss this matter or if there is any additional information you need.

Yours truly,

[Your signature]

[Your name printed]

Sample Notice Of Death –Credit Card Company

[Your name]
[Address line 1]
[Address line 2]
[E-mail address]
[Telephone No.]

[Date]

[Credit card company name]
[Address line 1]
[Address line 2]

Re: [name of deceased], Notice of Death ~~and Request for Information~~

Account number(s) [account number(s)]

To Whom It May Concern:

I am the executor of the estate of [deceased] who died on [date]. Please find enclosed a copy of the death certificate and a copy of the legal document proving my authority as the deceased's executor.

I request that you add a formal death notice to the credit file of the deceased. In addition, please inform me of the following as soon as possible:

- The current balance on the account(s) and the balance on the date of the deceased's death.
- Any other accounts the deceased has with your institution or affiliates.

Please do not hesitate to contact me to discuss this matter or if there is any additional information you need.

Yours truly,

[Your signature]

[Your name printed]

Sample Notice Of Death –Utility Company

[Your name]
[Address line 1]
[Address line 2]
[Telephone No.]
[E-mail address]

[Date]

[Name of Utility]
[Address line 1]
[Address line 2]

Re: [name of deceased], Notice of Death and Request
Account number: [account number]

To Whom It May Concern:

I am the executor of the estate of [deceased] who died on [date]. Please find enclosed a copy of the death certificate and a copy of the legal document proving my authority as the deceased's executor.

Revise as is applicable to your situation.

The landline telephone and internet account were in the deceased's name. I am still living in the property and would like to have the landline and internet account transferred into my own name.

The deceased also had a cell phone account in the deceased's name. Please disconnect this service and arrange for the final account to be forwarded to me.

If there are any forms or other documents that you require to transfer the landline and internet accounts to me or to disconnect the cell phone account, please send them to me.

Please do not hesitate to contact me to discuss this matter or if there is any additional information you need.

Yours truly,

[Your signature]

[Your name printed]

Sample Notice Of Death –Credit Reporting Agency

[Your name]
[Address line 1]
[Address line 2]
[Telephone No.]
[E-mail address]

[Date]

[Name of Credit Reporting Agency]
   [Address line 1]
   [Address line 2]

Re: [name of deceased], Notice of Death and Request for Information
   Account number(s) [account number(s)]

To Whom It May Concern:

I am the executor of the estate of [deceased] who died on [date]. Please find enclosed a copy of the death certificate and a copy of the legal document proving my authority as the deceased's executor.

I request that you add a formal death notice to the credit file of the deceased and a notation not to issue credit. In addition, please provide me with a copy of the deceased's current credit report.

Please do not hesitate to contact me to discuss this matter or if there is any additional information you need.

Yours truly,

[Your signature]

[Your name printed]

Sample Notice Of Death – Mortgage Lender

[Your name]
[Address line 1]
[Address line 2]
[Telephone No.]
[E-mail address]

[Date]

[Name of Mortgage Lender]
[Address line 1]
[Address line 2]

Re: [name of deceased], Notice of Death and Request for Information
Account number: [account number]

To Whom It May Concern:

I am the executor of the estate of [deceased] who died on [date]. Please find enclosed a copy of the death certificate and a copy of the legal document proving my authority as the deceased's executor.

Please inform me of the following as soon as possible:

- The current balance on the account and the amount of interest due as of the date of death.
- The amount of any upcoming payment and the due date for the payment.

Please do not hesitate to contact me to discuss this matter or if there is any additional information you need.

Yours truly,

[Your signature]

[Your name printed]

Sample Notice Of Death –Pension Provider

[Your name]
[Address line 1]
[Address line 2]
[Telephone No.]
[E-mail address]

[Date]

[Name of Pension Provider]
   [Address line 1]
   [Address line 2]

Re: [name of deceased], Notice of Death and Request for Information
   Account number: [account number]

To Whom It May Concern:

I am the executor of the estate of [deceased] who died on [date]. Please find enclosed a copy of the death certificate and a copy of the legal document proving my authority as the deceased's executor.

Please inform me of the following as soon as possible:

- The current balance and value of the deceased's pension.
- The survivor pension or other benefits for the deceased's beneficiaries payable now or in the future.
- The method for accessing the pension account and benefits.
- A copy of the pension and all related documents.

Please do not hesitate to contact me to discuss this matter or if there is any additional information you need.

Yours truly,

[Your signature]

[Your name printed]

Made in the USA
Columbia, SC
01 June 2023

17554073R00096